Place of the Skull

Best Regards,
Alan Fitzpatrick

D1376956

Place of the Skull

The Untold Story of Wheeling's Earliest History

By Alan Fitzpatrick

Cover Artwork: "Weel-lunk, Place of the Skull", oil on canvas by Cecy Rose.

To

Margaret Brennan

Wheeling's Historian

Other Books by the Author

Wilderness War on the Ohio

In Their Own Words

Table of Contents

Introduction

A philosopher friend of mine once wrote, "Under the beautiful lawn are millions of bodies who cavorted thereon." If only those lawns could speak might they divulge the secrets buried with those bones and the mysteries that could be solved with evidence finally brought to light. There is a mystery surrounding Wheeling, West Virginia's earliest history that persists to this day. It is a mystery that predates the arrival of the Zane family from Virginia in 1769 and the building of Fort Henry in 1774. These two events are generally accepted by historians as the beginning of Wheeling's history during the colonial frontier period. But this is not so. There is a mystery that has not been adequately investigated or solved for over two hundred and fifty years because few people have comprehended the nature of the mystery, and fewer still have grappled with it, and asked the right questions. What is this mystery? It begins with the meaning of the name of Wheeling. What does the name mean? Why was Wheeling given this name, and by whom, and for what reason? Therein lays the door to the mystery.

Wheeling is not named after a person. It is an English language word that is a corruption of an Indian word. The Indian word is an Indian place-name that dates back to the 18th Century, prior to Wheeling's colonial history beginning in 1769. The Delaware Indians, prior to the arrival of the Zanes, called the place where the creek flowed into the Ohio River, "Weel-lunk or Wihl-link," as it was phonetically written in English by 18th Century white men familiar with the Delaware language. Weel-lunk means or translates literally in the Delaware tongue to, "Place of the Scalped Head," otherwise called "Place of the Skull." However, research

9

has shown that the Delaware were not the first Indians to designate the locality as Place of the Skull. The Delaware were only taking an Iroquois word, "Kanororan" and translating that word into their own language as Weel-lunk. The mouth of the creek had already been named by the Iroquois prior to the arrival of the Delaware who migrated from eastern Pennsylvania, beginning in the 1740's.

The mystery deepens with this fact that the Delaware did not give Wheeling its original place-name. Some Delaware Indians whom Moravian preacher John Heckewelder ministered to, told him that it was a white man's scalped head which had been severed and placed upon a pole at the site of Weel-lunk; hence the place-name. Who, then, was this white man? The question has never been asked. The individual Indians told Heckewelder that the victim was a prisoner from one of their past wars. They were clearly wrong. Without a written history to quote from, they were merely recalling what they remembered from stories that had been told as oral history. The fact is that the Iroquois predated the naming of the creek to before the arrival of the Delaware and any white settlers to the Ohio Country, specifically the upper Ohio River Valley. The creek was named by the Iroquois before the French and Indian War which began in 1755 which the Delaware took part in. Surprisingly, the creek was already named before the expedition of the French military Celeron de Blainville in 1749, during which he stopped at the creek and buried a lead plate on the north bank at its mouth on the Ohio River.

If the creek was named by the Iroquois prior to 1749, then the white man had not been killed by the Delaware, as they supposed, but by the Iroquois themselves. By the time Celeron arrived at the mouth of

Wheeling Creek in August of 1749, the severed scalped head of a white man placed upon a pole had already decayed and fallen, or Celeron and his French priest, Bonnecamps, would surely have made note of its discovery in their journals. They did not. However, they did record the Iroquois name for the creek as Kanororan, which translated, means Place of the Skull. Evidently, the Iroquois accompanying the Celeron expedition were reluctant to translate the meaning of the creek name for a reason. Something had happened on the banks of that creek which had special significance to the Iroquois that they were not about to discuss with the white emissaries. The place meant more than the Place of the Skull to the Iroquois. It meant the place of evil; white man's evil.

What happened at the Place of the Skull to give it its name and special meaning that the Iroquois would not talk about? The aim of this book is to address this mystery and answer the questions of what happened in Wheeling's earliest history that made a lasting impression on all 18th Century Indians in the Ohio Country until their expulsion from Indian lands by 1800. Part One of this book is an in-depth look at the existing historical evidence and reference that gives key clues. The narrative of Part Two is an understanding of 18th Century Woodland Indian culture of the time, that is essential is seeing the events that happened through their eyes to intimately understand what happened and why. Part Three thoroughly examines the question of why, with historical evidence and cultural reference to Indian spiritual and religious beliefs and practices. Part Four deals with the lasting legacy of the event that has persisted by way of the name, which all Indians of the Ohio Country came to know thereof, even when most had never visited the Place of the Skull. The name Weel-lunk had special meaning only to Indians; not whites.

The place-name held significance to all Indians when the word was spoken. It was much like the 20th Century place-name of the Polish village, "Auschwitz." Although I have never been there, I know when I hear the name that it is associated with something of great evil that happened there to Jewish people during World War II. Though the word Auschwitz does not literally translate to the Place of the Murdered Jewish People, as Weel-lunk translated to Indians as the Place of the Skull, its name is no less associated with a horrible, tragic event that all who lived through that time period, and for generations to come, would understand. So it was with the place-name, Weel-lunk, now called Wheeling. Over forty years later after the event happened at Wheeling to give it its name, Indians in the Ohio Country, some more than two hundred miles away and a generation removed from the time of the actual event, were aware that Weel-lunk was a place of white man's evil perpetrated against Indians. The legacy of a cursed place was cemented in Indians' minds by subsequent proof validated during the years of warfare on the frontier that followed.

This, then, is the untold story of Wheeling's earliest history—the place of infamy to Indians in the Ohio Country in the 18th Century—the Place of the Skull.

"Place of the Skull," oil painting by Cecy Rose.

Part One:
The History

Place of the Skull

Chapter 1: A Place in the Ohio Country

It is difficult for us to imagine the vast inland aboriginal forest that once covered the interior of North America prior to the arrival of Europeans. Stretching from the crests of the Allegheny Mountains in the east, west to the Illinois Country and the Mississippi River lay an enormous, seemingly impenetrable land of unbroken original growth woodland. There were no roads, towns, or cultivated farmland; no fences, shopping malls or factories. It was a veritable wilderness; an endless forest that was broken only by the mighty Ohio River and its tributaries and covering much of what is today western Pennsylvania, Ohio, Indiana and Kentucky. To the white men who would eventually come to explore it, the land beyond the mountains hemming in the east coast of America appeared as nothing less than an unknown, forbidding wilderness beyond what any man of that time could comprehend. Collectively, those few men who attempted to transverse it beginning in the late 1600's would come to call it simply, the Ohio Country.

The Allegheny Mountains rose in the east parallel to the Atlantic coast, and provided a stunning natural barrier to the Ohio Country, serving as its eastern border. These mountains covered much of the mid-section of what we today call Pennsylvania, Maryland, West Virginia, and Virginia. The Alleghenies are part of a series of eroded uplifts from an ancient mountain range called the Appalachian Mountains that stretched from Georgia and the Carolinas to New York, New Hampshire and Vermont. They make up much of the central part of the greater Appalachians, and in essence, are a rugged series of steep parallel ridges forming individual ranges, all aligning in a general southwest to northeast direction for several hundred miles. Those ridges and their peaks rise as high as 3000 feet above sea level, with some towering above four thousand feet. These mist-covered heights are composed of massive rock and mineral escarpments that are highly resistant to weathering; thus, in effect, very old imposing natural barriers to westward land travel for man and beast alike for millennia.

Dramatically rising on the east side of the mountains, the Alleghenies begin with a high, steep uplifted ridge called the Allegheny Front that appears in most part, unbroken as far as the eye can see. From there westward, the Alleghenies rise and fall in a series of parallel mountain ridges with rolling valleys in between the ridges that are in some places several miles wide. These mountain ridges were given names by early explorers and settlers who followed. Broad Mountain and Cove Mountain form part of the immediate Allegheny Front in the east, with Kittatinny and Tuscarora Mountain lying behind them. Farther to the west, after crossing a broad rolling-hilled valley lays Sideling Hill Mountain parallel to the previous. Tussey, Evitts, Wills and Buffalo Mountains follow. Chestnut Ridge Mountain is the last large imposing mountain ridge making up the west side of the Alleghenies. From there, the Alleghenies gradually gives way to less imposing Laurel Ridge and its accompanying highlands. These Laurel Highlands are made up of a series of descending ridges and uplands that undulate all the way to the Ohio River. Cut into them are the major tributaries of the Ohio: the Allegheny, Monongahela and Youghiogheny Rivers and their individual watersheds that drain the west side of the Alleghenies to the Ohio and beyond.

The Allegheny mountain ridges were virtually impenetrable to early exploration if not for a handful of creeks and streams draining them that cut gaps through the ridges and between them. These natural gaps allowed not only for the passage of water, but also the migrations of herds of deer, elk, and eastern bison that followed the waterways as they wound their way through the mountains. The long, lazy Susquehanna River flowing in a south-easterly direction east of the Alleghenies to Chesapeake Bay and the Atlantic had several tributaries that fed the Susquehanna from the Alleghenies. Chief among these mountain rivers was the meandering Juniata River that begins in the heart of the Alleghenies and winds its way from many branches until it emerges north of what is now Harrisburg. It would be streams and creeks like that of the Juniata that Woodland Indians would follow for generations prior to the coming of the white man. They would use the mountain trails for the purposes of hunting, trading, and most importantly, making war upon their enemies.

The Allegheny Mountains were originally covered with thick aboriginal forest. The mist-shrouded valleys between the ridge heights were heavily wooded with stands of old-growth cedar, hemlock, oak, hickory, chestnut, maple, poplar, elm, beech and spruce that towered high above the narrow trails winding through them below. As the mountains gave way at last to the Laurel Highlands, the Allegheny uplift began its gentle long rolling descent to the Ohio River. Here, the Ohio Country truly began. The endless hardwood forest was well-watered with a more temperate climate than the mountains, so the forest grew to heights beyond anything seen today. Trees towered more than a hundred feet into the air, their limbs reaching out to the sky in an interlocking fashion that allowed little sunlight to reach the forest floor. Trunks of these trees were many feet in diameter. They had stood for several centuries untouched by axe or saw. The animal, and then human paths that wound their way beneath the forest canopy traversing around massive tree trunks and their roots were hardly more than a couple of feet wide. In most places the trails were barely traceable in the gloom of the forest floor because only a fraction of daylight reached the ground, due to the imposing tree canopy above.

To the northwest of the Alleghenies lay the Great Lakes, a vast natural connecting water-way that bordered the mountains. The five enormous lakes drain eastward and eventually form the St. Lawrence River that flows to the Atlantic Ocean. To the southwest of the Alleghenies lay more open, rolling lands that comprised part of the Ohio Country. It would come to be known as Kentucky to whites and Indians alike. Here the heavy forest began to break with intermittent grasslands that native Indians expanded upon by yearly burnings, so that grass forage would grow and attract animals that could be hunted. Consequently, the lands south of the Ohio River, drained by rivers that flowed into the Ohio, became the ancestral hunting grounds for indigenous peoples that migrated to and from the area prior to the arrival of white men. Herds of elk, eastern bison, deer, and all sorts of waterfowl were plentiful to be hunted for their meat and skins. Other fur-bearing animals were also in abundance, including the beaver and the bear. To the north of the Ohio River, in the heart of the Ohio Country, animal herds were plentiful as well, making the land to the west of the Alleghenies rich in wildlife, and resources for the taking that Indian tribes could thrive upon.

Bisecting the Ohio Country nearly in half, and at the same time tying it intricately together with a web of tributaries was the large river that would be called by the Iroquois, "Ohi:yo" meaning, the "great river, the good river." Stretching over nine hundred miles from the headwaters of what is now known as the Allegheny River, The Ohio wound its way gently to the southwest. It skirted the edge of the Allegheny Highlands to the east, and divided them from the rolling hills slipping off to the west that extended to the heart of the Ohio Country. Here, the Ohio would be strengthened by the binding together of three rivers before making a turn first west, then southwest, and finally to the west again to meet the grand Mississippi River in Illinois Country as its largest tributary. It is generally accepted that the Frenchman, Rene-Robert Cavalier, Sieur de La Salle, was the first white man to travel the Ohio River and view the adjoining Ohio Country. Born in Normandy, France, in 1743 and arriving in Canada after leaving the Jesuit education, La Salle established a home on the island in the St. Lawrence River at the fledgling New France village of Montreal he called "La Chine," meaning China. However, La Salle yearned for adventure and put together the means to fulfill his desire for exploration to discover a waterway route to China and the Orient. He kept no journal of his expeditions into the interior of America. Some historians doubt that he made the trip to the Ohio Country at all, and returned to Montreal after being discouraged by the Iroquois in 1669 from entering the lands that they recently claimed by conquest. [1]

Regardless, it has been generally accepted that La Salle made his first exploratory expedition from New France in 1669, and headed for the lands south of the Great Lakes that were rumored by the Huron to hold a great river route to the ocean. The idea tantalized La Salle's imagination since he had first heard of the great river from Seneca Indians, "who had come to Montreal in the autumn of the year 1668 to do their hunting and trading." [2] La Salle consulted the Jesuit Abbe Gallinee to ask the Senecas if they could provide a prisoner from the Ohio Country as a guide, which they were able to do once La Salle and his party arrived in Seneca country. Gallinee, with another Jesuit Abbe Dollier, were headed to the Lake Erie region and beyond, and agreed to accompany La Salle and his men as far as the Seneca villages below Lake Ontario. [3] Said Gallinee, "Our fleet consisted of seven canoes, each manned by three men, which departed Montreal the sixth day of July, 1669, under the guidance of two canoes of Iroquois Sonnontoueronons (Senecas.)" [4] La Salle and his party arrived by boat on the southeastern shore of Lake Erie after having ascended the St. Lawrence River to Lake Ontario, and portaged around Niagara Falls that took him to the next great lake. There, after leaving the Jesuits, they were met by a number of Iroquois Indians who demanded to know who La Salle was and what his intentions were. It quickly became evident to the Iroquois headmen that La Salle was French, and therefore an unwelcome intruder to the lands which the Iroquois had recently acquired through conquest from the former inhabitants, the Eries, and others. La Salle petitioned to them that he was not an enemy; only a friendly visitor from New France wishing to bring trade goods to them. However, the Iroquois were not so sure, and no doubt decided to hold a council without La Salle and his men present, to decide what to do with the obvious French interlopers.

Likely, the Seneca headmen each had a say in the deliberations as they smoked their pipes of tobacco in a bark-covered wigwam shelter set up for that purpose. Many advised that the Frenchmen should be put to death for their intransigence, as they were enemies of all Iroquois. The headmen knew that they were at the height of their empire, and needed to bargain or negotiate with no one, least of all this pitiful handful of French men, whose scalps had more value than the paltry trade goods they offered as gifts. The people called the *Erielhonan* or *Erie* living on the lands south of the lake later given their name were the latest to know the might of the Iroquois who had all but exterminated them for accepting refugees from Huron villages that the Iroquois had destroyed. Too, many tribes to the south in the Ohio Country had been driven to the west by the Iroquois who feared no one. To the north, their hated enemies, the Huron, were conquered and dispersed. Their French allies had been rebuked with guns procured through trade with the Dutch in Albany. So as the Iroquois headmen sat in council, they did so with the knowledge that their own appetite for French blood had been sated with the blood of French men in retribution for the many the outrages committed against their own people in the past. The wrongs of the French had been avenged, though not forgotten. Deep in the heart of every warrior, he knew that blood must be answered with blood. His reputation, his honor, and hence that of his family, his clan, his tribe and all his people hung on fulfilling vengeance, even if at the cost of his own life. And once a people became an enemy of the Iroquois, each and every one of them would be considered an enemy without distinction.

However, the council ended with cooler heads prevailing. They reminded those seated that a treaty of peace had been signed with the French only four years before, and with the words of the treaty still as binding as the belts of wampum that had been exchanged, for the moment it would be foolish, if not dangerous, for them to dispose of the Frenchmen without proper consent from the elders of all the Five Nations. It was finally agreed that the French man La Salle and his pitifully small and under armed party would be allowed to live. La Salle was to be counseled one more time to give up his venture. However, if he insisted on leaving, the Iroquois would allow him and his men to pass unmolested this time only until the matter could be properly brought up at the council fire at Onondaga. Besides, several of them had developed an amusement, if not fondness for the audacious and foolish French captain, if for nothing more than his seemingly complete ignorance of his reckless, precarious position among the Iroquois which at any moment could cost him and his men their lives. Too, the Iroquois noted with interest that La Salle told them that he had once been a Black Robe. He said that he had discarded his Black Robe forever so as to become a real man and a warrior. The Iroquois considered what La Salle said, and liked it. To them, the Black Robes were like foolish carping women. The Iroquois were well-acquainted with the hated Jesuit missionaries who had brought disease and an alien religion to their villages throughout Iroquoia. The Indians had tortured the priests and burned them alive to test whether their Christian god would save them. Their god had not interfered with their deaths; yet the Iroquois had developed a begrudging respect for the robed men who sacrificed themselves so easily without begging for mercy. This man before them named La Salle claimed himself to have been one of them, and they believed him.

La Salle and his party were allowed to leave. Through an Indian interpreter who promised to guide them to the great river to the south, La Salle and his men portaged overland south from Lake Erie, entering the

Ohio Country by way of a tributary of the Mahoning River, and to a waterway that he was told the Iroquois called "Ohi:yo." Here La Salle and his party of men in nine canoes descended the river that was a major waterway flowing to the southwest. To La Salle, the "Ohi:yo" was indeed a "great river; a good river," and much more. Its waters teemed with fish, fowl and wildlife the likes of which La Salle had not seen in Canada. He was amazed at what he saw on the upper reaches of the Ohio which was later to be called the Allegheny River. To La Salle it was a beautiful river, so he himself named it, "La Belle Riviere, The Beautiful River," claiming all the land that the river drained for France. The tributaries of the Ohio La Salle noted, as they passed by, were big and small, and entered the Ohio from both the east and the west. However, paramount in making the Ohio a great river was the joining of it with two major tributaries each of considerable size, at a place which would come to be known as the "Forks of the Ohio," at present day Pittsburgh. Here, the Allegheny River flowing from the north joined the Monongahela River from the south and the Youghiogheny River from the southeast, each fed by its own network of tributary streams originating in the Alleghenies. As La Salle and his men beached their canoes on the spit of land squeezed between the three colliding rivers La Salle noted to himself that this key forks could someday be a strategic outpost for France.

From the Forks of the Ohio, the river made a significant turn to the west for several miles. Along the banks at intervals, La Salle observed evidence of the presence of Indians living in hunting camps and semi-permanent minor villages on both sides of the river. The Ohio was obviously a major water transportation route for Indians by canoe, and must have

25

been for some time until the Iroquois had usurped the local tribes and now claimed the river and its surrounding land as their own once the local populations had been dispersed or killed. With equal interest, La Salle must have taken notice of the river itself. Perhaps he took soundings from time to time to note the river's depth. Never deep, the Ohio, at points, ran as shallow as three feet up to twenty feet, depending upon the time of year and the natural watershed runoff. There were probably places where La Salle's canoes scraped river bottom or hidden sandbars, in spite of the best efforts of his men to keep to the main river channel. Evident to La Salle was the difference between the Ohio and the rivers he was acquainted with in Canada, such as the St. Lawrence and the Ottawa. The Ohio was never more than a quarter mile wide, and bottom land on either side of the river was in most places narrow compared to the wide land bordering the St. Lawrence, La Salle noted. This was because of the fairly abrupt rise of sizable bluffs and steep hills from which the Ohio had cut through. Those ridged-hills appeared to be more than one or two hundred feet in height over the river itself.

At a point nearly thirty miles from the forks, the Ohio began its bend roughly to the southwest following this course for a great distance through the trackless wooded wilderness of the Ohio Country. Day after day, La Salle and his men paddled on, until reaching a sizable cataract in the river that would come to be called the "Falls of the Ohio River" at what is now Louisville, Kentucky. It was here that La Salle's men collectively had had enough of the endless sojourn. They demanded to turn back for Canada with or without La Salle himself, rather than continue further down the river which seemed to have no end. Reluctantly, La Salle agreed, and was forced to turn around and return the way they had come. Further exploration would have to wait for another day, and one can only imagine what La Salle thought returning up the "beautiful river." However disappointed he was, La Salle, in his favor, had noted many interesting things that caught his eye which he would not forget. He had passed a multitude of rivers emptying into the Ohio such as the Kanawha, Muskingum, Hockhocking, Scioto, and Miami. These rivers, though unnamed at the time, showed evidence of Indian habitation at their mouths, and more intriguing, when La Salle and his men camped on the banks of these rivers draining from the Ohio Country, though the village-like bark huts and hunting camps were abandoned, well-used trails led away from them along the river banks into the interior land. La Salle could see that were used regularly not only by animals but by human feet, Indian feet.

One such place must have caught La Salle's attention on either the trip down the Ohio or the trip back. An unnamed creek flowed into the Ohio River from the east which was one of many countless streams that emptied into the Ohio from the bottom of runs or gullies worn into the surrounding hills. The mouth of this particular creek was approximately ninety miles downriver from the forks of the Ohio. It was non-descript and La Salle and his men would have hardly noticed the creek and stopped by it, if not for a unique feature. Opposite the mouth of the creek lay a sizable island in the middle of the Ohio that effectively split the river into two channels. The island itself was one of only a handful that La Salle and his party had passed on their exploratory journey. It was the island that made the north bank of the creek an attractive site for halting to camp. The shallows in the Ohio River adjacent the island made it the home for numerous game animals to forage

27

off the lush island vegetation. The deer and elk could be easily hunted because they could not escape quickly if they plunged into the moving water of the Ohio on either side, which would slow them down. On the north bank of the creek opposite the east side of the island, La Salle likely found evidence of an Indian hunting camp, and more. A well-used path led away from the Ohio heading east, following the north bank of the creek as it wound through the bottom lands into the interior.

Perhaps La Salle found the remains of pole drying racks erected for curing meat and dressing hides. Fire pits lined with stones would have been present, along with evidence of temporary bark lean-to shelters. Mixed in with any debris La Salle would have noticed broken stone arrow heads and spear points, with flakes of flint indicating that Indians had paused at this camping site to make new points over the years. In fact, later explorers and settlers to the area would document the continual habitation of the Ohio River Valley by Indian tribes pre-dating La Salle's expedition and Iroquois expansion by hundreds and hundreds of years, calling them Adena and Hopewell cultures. The well-used trail itself was evident of continual use. Perhaps no wider than one man could travel on, the path was used often enough to cause a slight depression in the ground that one could trace with the eye. La Salle did not choose to follow the trail, not knowing where it led, other than comprehending that it would take him away from the Ohio River and the relative safety of his canoes. In years to come long after La Salle's visit, other white men would find this path used by Indians of the Ohio Country. The path would take the name The Mingo Path. [5] It would be recognized that it took travelers east along adjacent creek watersheds to the Monongahela River, and to trails that led in all directions, north, south and further east. What La Salle may not have understood was that all creeks and streams flowing into the Ohio River had paths of their own that Indians followed. As the water ways themselves connected the Ohio River to that the land that it drained so did the network of walk-ways join the people to the land.

If La Salle had looked further, he might have found that the path at the mouth of the creek did not end on the banks of the Ohio. It was not a lone terminus as he suspected, but part of a larger continuous east-west trail. It crossed the river and continued west after fording the shallows on either side of the island, adjacent to the mouth of the creek. Crossing the west channel of the Ohio, the path picked up again just north of another creek mouth flowing into the Ohio from the west, almost opposite to the creek entering the Ohio from the east. There, the path followed the north bank of the creek west into the heartland of the Ohio Country [6] and was joined by adjacent trails merging with it from the northwest, where Indians from the Great Lakes region or from the far west interior could travel east and ultimately to the Atlantic coast or the Carolinas. That main east-west Indian trail would later be called by many the "Old Mingo Trail" and would one day be widened by white men and eventually become a major road for westward travel long after the expulsion of all Indians. [7]

Did La Salle, while pausing at this undistinguished creek, see into its future? Likely not. Was there any sentient feeling hidden by the blandness of the forest serving as a backdrop to the remains of the Indian hunting camp on the north bank of the creek that could be picked up by a sensitive soul? Indians held great regard for sentient feelings as harbingers of things to come or things past that they believed white man's minds were closed to. La Salle, with his limited

29

experience in dealing with Indians, would not have known what to look for or listen to, even if his mind was open to such things. His Iroquois Indian guide, on the other hand, would have. From the time he was old enough to understand, he would have been schooled in the art of sensing and feeling things that were not evident, clear, or visible. His inner eye would be looking for signs—what some whites would call intuitions that would lead his mind to question if something about a particular place or situation did not feel right. What was it that stopped him for a moment, to pause and listen on the banks of this particular creek? Was it a sighing in the wind, a rustle in the leaves, or the lapping of creek water on stones? Something did not feel right about this place, he felt, causing him to ask to himself if it was something that already happened, or would happen. A passing raven cawed. Something yet to happen was the answer he heard. Immediately the Indian turned his head away from the creek and closed his mind to this silent enquiry and response. The foreboding he clearly felt made him shudder with the conviction that he did not want to know more.

La Salle and his men had no inkling of the deed that would be committed at this place. They would not know of the dark pall cast over this spot that all Indians of the Ohio Country would come to know of and understand, even though most Indians would never see this place with their own eyes. Too, future generations of Indians who knew nothing of the specifics would implicitly understand the significance of the name that would be given to this spot and what happened here. It would be a name that was more a feeling for an event than a place; and a reminder, not a warning, as whites would later believe. All Indians would know what the French men and other whites to follow would not comprehend—that on the creek bank by a particular island in the Ohio River an evil act had been perpetrated by evil white men against Indians, and revenge had been sought to right the grievous wrong committed. Blood had been answered with blood, and flesh with flesh for it. Vengeance had been fulfilled, and this was not ever to be forgotten, as the name would imply as a reminder to all Indians. Not a name meaning a warning to one's enemies, but a name invoking the testament to this place of bad medicine. "Kanororan, in Iroquois. Weel-lunk in Delaware. Wheeling in English." This was the name given to a place like no other name in America: "Place of the Scalped Head, the Skull, and He whose spirit wanders eternally."

Place of the Skull

Chapter 2: The People of the Longhouse

The Iroquois did not call themselves by the name given to them by the French, their enemy in Canada. Some say that the French referred to them as *irinakhoiw*, a Huron word that means "black snakes," and from thence, Iroquois. The Huron to the north were ancestral enemies of the Iroquois who allied themselves with the French when they arrived in the New World. Others believe that the French adopted the word "hilokoa," another Algonquin word which means "killer people" to describe the hostile Indian nation to the south of the St. Lawrence River and the French colony of New France. In any case, "Iroquois" was an insulting, derogatory word name that they did not recognize or acknowledge. Rather, the fitting name for what was to become a unique league was, "Ganonsyoni" and "Haudenosaunee," meaning, "People of the Lodge that is spread out far," thus, "The People of the Longhouse." The Haudenosaunee did not exist as a united league of tribes until an important event occurred sometime between 1450 and 1600. It was then that five distinct tribes of Indians living in the area of what is now upstate New York, stretching from the eastern shores of Lake Erie to the Hudson River, united as one. Oral tradition and legend tells the story of their unusual unification.

According to the oral story that was told for generations by the story tellers of the Haudenosaunee, there once were five separate tribes of loosely-related Indian peoples who "shared a common ancestry and similar language." They lived adjacent to each other in lands south of Lake Ontario in the 1400's. The *Kanien'keha:ka*, or "People of the Great Flint" lived the furthermost east of all five tribes along the Mohawk

River from which they would take their English name, "Mohawk Indians." Next to them to the west were the *Onayotekaono*, or "People of the Standing Stone," on the shores of Oneida Lake, from which they would derive their English name, Oneida Indians. In the center of the five tribes, to the west of Lake Oneida were the Ononda'gega, or "People of the Hills," close to Onondaga Lake from which they would be called Onondaga Indians and "Keepers of the League's Fire." West of the Onondagas were the *Guyohkohnyoh*, or "People of the Great Swamp." They resided at the vicinity of Cayuga Lake from which they would take their English name, Cayuga Indians. And finally, on the west of the five tribes lived the tribe called *Onondaga*, or "People of the Great Hill" in the area of Seneca Lake and the Genesee River. Not to be confused with the Onondaga tribe, the "People of the Great Hill," the largest of the five tribes in population would take the English name, the Seneca. Much later, in 1722, a sixth tribe would be added to the Haudenosaunee named the *Ska-Ruh-Reh*, or "Hemp Gatherers" who were a tribe from the North Carolina region who petitioned to join the League of Five Nations already in existence. They would be known as the Tuscarora.

These original five tribes were distinct from each other and constantly squabbling among themselves over land, water, and hunting rights. The constant feuding which often led to violent conflict was an intolerable condition that none of them could ill-afford, with Algonquin enemies to the north waging intermittent warfare against them, and the hostile Susquahannocks, Catawba, and Cherokee tribes to the south who were raiding their lands. However, sometime after 1450, an adopted Huron Indian of the Onondaga tribe who claimed to be a prophet and spiritual leader proposed a novel idea to the Onondaga council of elders that no one had previously considered. Deganawidah, called "The Great Peacemaker," brought a message to the council known as the "Great Law of Peace." Oral tradition tells that the Huron, Deganawidah, "left his homeland for Iroquoia, where he found the people torn apart by war. Deganawidah traveled about, preaching his message of peace. His most important convert was Hiawatha, an Onondaga who had killed and eaten many of his enemies but whose grief over the loss of his own daughters left him inconsolable. Deganawidah restored Hiawatha's well-being by giving him three strings of wampum beads while reciting words of condolence. One string dried Hiawatha's tears so that he might see clearly again. Another cleared his throat, so that he could speak, and the last opened his ears, so that he could hear. Deganawidah taught the sacred words and use of the sacred beads to Hiawatha, who used them to spread the prophet's message of peace." [8]

Oral tradition tells that Hiawatha was a skilled and charismatic orator of the Onondaga tribe. He spoke for Deganawidah before an assembled council of the headmen of all five nations who had been called by the Onondaga elders to hear what Hiawatha had to say. Deganawidah himself was not allowed to speak before the council because he was Huron. Other accounts suggest that in addition to his Huron blood that Deganawidah had a speak impediment as well. Hiawatha, in his stead, proposed that the five tribes unite in lasting peace to become one nation composed of five separate ones, who would support and defend each other against all others, and never pick up the war hatchet against any one of the five. It is said that Hiawatha presented a persuasive argument for unification by holding up to the council five individual sticks that could easily be broken in half one at a time, representing the five nations present. Then holding up five new unbroken sticks that were this time held together as one with binding, Hiawatha demonstrated that the strength of five sticks bound together could not be broken. His persuasive argument was compelling, and the League of Five Nations, to be called the "People of the Long House," the Haudenosaunee, was formed. The Seneca to the west would be called the "People of the Western Gate" and the Mohawk to the east would be known as the "People of the Eastern Gate." It was agreed that the Onondagas in the center would serve as the "Keepers of the Council Fire" of the Haudenosaunee. It was vowed that all would come to each other's aid if any of the five were attacked by enemies, solidifying the conviction that an enemy of any of the five was now an enemy of all.

The name "People of the Long House" derived from the manner in which the Haudenosaunee built their homes in the 1600's, which was similar to their Algonquin enemies to the north. A good description can be found in the account of the French explorer Jacques Cartier in his 1535 journal entry of the village of Hochelaga on the island of Montreal in the St. Lawrence River which fit the descriptions given by later Jesuit missionaries to the Haudenosaunee in the 17th century. "The village is circular is completely enclosed by a wooden palisade in three tiers like a pyramid. The top one is built crosswise, the middle one perpendicular and the lowest one of strips of wood placed lengthwise....There are more than fifty houses in this village, each about fifty or more paces in length, and twelve or fifteen in width, built completely of wood and covered in and bordered up with large pieces of bark and rind of trees, as broad as a table, which are well and cunningly lashed after their manner. And inside these houses are many rooms and chambers; and in the middle is a large space without a floor, where they light their fire and live together in common." [9]

What the nations of the Haudenosaunee had been building were permanent fortified homes made of a wooden frame sheathed in sheets of tree bark to shed rain and snow. This traditional longhouse structure would still be found in the mid-1750's, and was not confined to the Haudenosaunee alone even when log cabin home-style building was adopted by many Indian tribes from the white frontier settlers. The Susquehannocks, enemies of the Haudenosaunee who lived in what is now central to south Pennsylvania and Maryland, likewise built longhouse structures inside forts. "The Susquehannocks lived in stockaded villages. Their typical longhouse, like that of the Iroquois north of them, was from sixty to eighty feet in length, having a door at each end." [10] A white captive of the Shawnee Indians remembers a visit to an Indian longhouse in the Ohio Country in 1788. "At length the old chief to whom I belonged, appeared and led me to his own house. This was about twenty feet long and fourteen feet wide, the sides and roof made of small pole and covered with bark. The entrance was at the end, and an old blanket hung in the doorway." [11] However, the Haudenosaunee longhouses were much longer and more elaborate. In 1653, a Dutch visitor to one of the Mohawk fortified villages, or "castles" noted a typical longhouse size and construction. "Their houses are mostly of one and the same shape, without any special embellishment or remarkable design. They sometimes build them as long as some hundred feet, though never more than twenty feet wide." [12] The reason the Haudenosaunee built a palisade wall around their village of longhouses was the same reason that the Huron to the north and the Susquehannocks to the south did—for protection, not from animal predators, but from the constant enemy war parties entering each other's territory to wage warfare that had been going on for generations immemorial.

As the Haudenosaunee League of Five Nations consolidated their political unification, they also underwent an intense period sharing everything else known amongst them in regards to living, from herbal medicine, child-rearing, cooking, hunting, and fishing techniques to the all-important primary agricultural techniques of their time. This would allow the Haudenosaunee to become highly successful farmers able to raise enough food to support a growing population, and provide the numbers of warriors necessary to expand their territory through sustained warfare. Consequently, by the early 1600's the Haudenosaunee as a whole became adept at growing crops of varieties of corn, beans and squash in amounts of food far greater than hunting could afford, thus making crop food their traditional main diet. The Haudenosaunee reflected upon their horticultural success by considering their three mainstay crops special gifts from the Creator, or Great Spirit, calling corn, beans and squash the "Three Sisters." Farming techniques were improved upon and shared by all. It was found that crops could be grown with design and scheme in mind. "The cornstalks grow, the bean plants climb the stalks, and the squash grow beneath, inhibiting weeds and keeping the soil moist under the shade of their broad leaves. In this combination, the soil remained fertile for several decades. The food was stored during the winter, and it lasted for two to three years." [13] As a result, the Haudenosaunee thrived, multiplied, and began to look beyond their own lands to expand, which could only come about by waging war.

Warfare had been an ingrained, endemic way of life for all Woodland Indian nations long before the arrival of whites and the Haudenosaunee were no exception. However, prior to unification of the five tribes, they had not fared well in warfare, and now, unified as one tribe and able to field a multitude of warriors into the field against their neighbors, the future promised to be brighter. What was to be gained by warfare? Defeating another tribe in battle meant that the victor, if possible, could plunder the vanquished tribe's village of foodstuffs, household goods, and most-importantly, captives of the enemy, especially women and children. In rare cases, adult male captives would be taken for adoption, but more than likely, if an enemy warrior was captured in battle, his naked body was painted black on return to the village, and he was tortured and burned alive, to satisfy collective vengeance for losses the village as a whole had sustained at the hands of the enemy tribe. Everyone in the village would partake in the sacrifice. It would begin upon the arrival of the returning war party. A description follows: "The Indians, men, women, and children collect together, bringing clubs and stones in order to beat them [the prisoner captives] which they usually do with great severity, by way of revenge for the relations who have been slain: this is performed immediately upon their entering the village where the warriors reside." [14] A white captive in 1755 remembered what happened. "The men and women came out to meet us and stripped me naked. After this, they pointed to a wigwam [long house] and told me to run to it. They beat me with sticks and stones all along the way." [15] This prisoner ritual was called later by whites, "running of the gauntlet."

Once the captive had successfully made their way through the gauntlet, the elders of the village decided the prisoner's fate on the spot. Would the captive be adopted by a family who had lost a loved one

39

in the war party, or serve as a slave for the village? Adoption was usually the preferred response for captured women and children. It would happen like this. Grieving families, called mourners in the village, would come forward to the captives who survived the gauntlet beating and petition their claims. "If they receive a prisoner, it is at their option either to satiate their vengeance by taking his life in the most cruel manner they can conceive of; or to receive and adopt him into the family, in the place of him whom they have lost." Once adopted into the tribe, the captive was considered a member of equal standing in the tribe. "Of the men, some are appointed to supply the places of such Indians as have fallen in battle. These are delivered to their friends and relations, and if they are received by them, they have no sufferings to fear; they are adopted into the family, and succeed to all the privileges of the deceased, and are esteemed as friends, brothers, and near relations." [16] Such was the adoption of enemy prisoners. As a period of sustained warfare began for the Haudenosaunee in 1609 that would last nearly a hundred years, adoptions served an essential purpose of bolstering their own tribal numbers, as well as dispersing the tribes that they were warring against by assimilating them directly into their own people. It is said that by the time of La Salle's expedition that nearly two thirds of the population in Oneida villages were former members of Algonquin and Huron Indians that they had been at war with.

If the captive was not considered fit for adoption, or if he were an enemy warrior captured in battle, then it was decided by the council of elders that he was to be tortured and burned as a sacrifice to appease the need for vengeance. Blood feuding and seeking revenge was an ingrained cultural fact of life for all Woodland Indian tribes both prior to the advent of

Europeans and long after their arrival. It was a tradition typical to all tribal peoples world-wide throughout history. The need to seek revenge for an injustice committed against one's family, clan, or tribe was a code of traditional laws that had been passed down orally for hundreds of years, and respected widely by all tribes. Fulfilling vengeance made a man gain honor in the face of his people, that was required for him to be a warrior. Without honor he was without a shadow and without dignity. It was expected of him to be brave in war; to kill many of the enemy, and to exact revenge even at the cost of his own life in trying to do so when the circumstances dictated so. Seeking revenge for wrongs committed gave rise to vendettas that lasted generations. That was one of the reasons for the formation of the Haudenosaunee League of Five Nations—to stop the divisive warfare between them that had devastated the warrior population of all of them. If a warrior's brother had been killed by a member of an enemy tribe, then the insult had to be avenged, and the duty of vengeance demanded an "eye for an eye," and fell upon the eldest brother of the family. However, a vengeance killing could be exacted upon any adult male of the tribe, not specifically the person in question who had originally committed the act. So faced with the murder of his kin, a warrior would demand vengeance which often led to wholesale war against all members of the enemy tribe. Consequently, seeking and fulfilling vengeance was on the top of the list of a warrior's priorities, and intimately tied to his psyche as warfare itself was.

When a prisoner from an enemy tribe was brought back to the home village and condemned to be burned, it was the intent of the tribe as a whole to seek vengeance upon the enemy for those who had been killed or captured by them in war. Rarely was it personal, and then only in cases where a captive had been adopted into a family and a conflict had resulted whereby the adoptee was considered unfit. Sometimes returning warriors painted captured enemy prisoners black, signifying they were to be burned for losses incurred on the raid, and so it would be done, unless the captive was specifically claimed by a widowed woman who requested the adoption of the prisoner to replace a dead husband. However, there were cases where the enemy warrior proved to be unsatisfactory as a husband after adoption, whereupon the woman would turn the man over to the tribe to be tortured and burned. Other cases of reneging on adoption occurred. "An Iroquois chief was reputed to have adopted and subsequently burned 40 prisoners because they did not prove worthy to succeed his dead brother." [17] Too, if a prisoner upon return to the home village was presented as a potential adoptee to a woman who had lost a husband or son; it was always requisite that she accept the adoptee first. A case was observed by white traders in a village. "The prisoner arrived, and was presented to the Half-king's wife, but she refused to accept him [as an adopted son] which, according to the Indian rule, was, in fact, a sentence of death. The young man was, therefore, taken away, for the purpose of being tortured and burnt on the pile." [18] When the decision was made to condemn the prisoner to death, he would be stripped naked, painted black from head to toe signifying death, and tied to a black-painted stake in the center of the village. The techniques of burning the prisoner were varied, however all gruesomely long and drawn out to evoke as much terrible pain as possible. The ritual involved the participation of everyone in the village, including children, and was viewed as a collective cleansing of the psyche of the tribe as a whole done by inflicting suffering on the enemy; in this case, the unfortunate individual representing that tribe.

This was the reason that the Haudenosaunee, as well as warriors from other Woodland tribes fought to the death in battle, rather than surrender and be captured. A warrior was trained to know what awaited him if he were captured. He knew it was better to die fighting to the absolute last of his will and strength than to be roasted on an enemy's spit. Rather, the warrior was educated to understand that among the men in his own tribe, "No one can arrive at any place of honor, among them but by merit," according to a white man James Smith who was captured by the Caughnawaga Iroquois and lived with them for several years. [19] Seeking and fulfilling vengeance was an important facet of a warrior's honor and served as the basis for garnering achievements for himself on the field of battle. "He who discovers most bravery in war, who has obtained the scalps of their enemies, or taken the greatest number of prisoners, received wounds, is honored by his countrymen. On the other hand, he who has never hazarded his life in the field, is dishonored by being called a woman, and esteemed of little worth," stated a missionary who lived with the Indians. [20] Seeking vengeance and making war upon an enemy were so hand-in-hand that the two were never considered as separate concepts among Indians, leading white men to conclude that vengeance was the main cause of all war. Said John Heckewelder, the 18th century Moravian minister who lived among the Indians of the Ohio country most of his life, "It is a fixed principle with the Indians, that evil cannot come out of good, that no friend will injure a friend, and therefore, that whoever wrongs or does harm to another is his ENEMY. As it is with individuals, so it is with nations and tribes. If they commit murder on another people, encroach on their lands, by making it a practice to come within their bounds and take the game from them, if they rob or steal from their hunting camps, or, in short, are guilty of any act of unjust aggression, they cannot be considered otherwise than as ENEMIES; they are declared to be such, and the aggrieved nation think themselves justifiable in punishing them." [21] But vengeance could also take the form of personal revenge of one upon another, on the individual level. Said Heckewelder, "If murder has been perpetrated, revenge is taken in the same way." [22]

For the Haudenosaunee, native society for the males focused solely upon seeking revenge and waging war upon their enemies, and to this end their culture revolved completely. Said a white man observing Woodland Indian habits, "Their souls are wholly bent upon war. This is what procures them glory among the men, and makes them the admiration of women. To this they are educated from the earliest youth." [23] Thus, warrior training began at a young age in the life of the male boy. He was schooled in the art of using weapons and the stratagem of hunting, upon which the techniques of warfare were based. Traditionally, men were not employed in cultivating crops, preparing food, or dressing hides. These domestic duties of Haudenosaunee life were assigned solely to the women, as the men engaged in hunting and fighting. Boys learning how to hunt game animals, learned at the same time, the wiles of hunting men in war. Another white observer of Indian warfare in the late 1600's, noted, "Their employment as hunters has taught the great address and vigilance in following and surprising game. Their mode of warfare is the same as that of hunting. With great ingenuity they will find and follow the track of their enemies; with a surprising patience and perseverance they will wait for the moment when they find him the least able to defend himself; and when they can find an enemy unprepared, they make their attack with great fury and with pretty sure success." [24] Young men schooled in this manner of waging war as an extension of hunting, developed skills based upon stealth, concealment, ambush, flanking maneuver, and surprise attack that unleashed ruthless, maximum violence upon an unsuspecting enemy who were, in most cases, out-maneuvered and out-numbered. Again, vengeance was at the heart of warfare, and once the attack began, vengeance was about to be fulfilled. Describing what happens when Indians attack from ambush, Samuel Williams in the late 1600's Vermont said, "The Indians immediately come forward, and begin the scene of outrage and death. All is then a scene of fury, impetuosity, and vengeance. So great is the rage of the savage, that he has no regard for discipline, subordination, and order. Revenge takes an entire possession of his soul; forgetful of all order, regardless of discipline and danger, he aims only to butcher and destroy." [25]

Place of the Skull

Chapter 3: The Haudenosaunee Pick up the War Hatchet

Beginning at the turn of the 17th century, the Haudenosaunee turned their attention towards the north, and the tribes living there that were ancestral enemies of the Five Nations. This included the Huron, Algonquin, Montagnais, and Etechemin living along the St. Lawrence River valley and north of Lake Ontario, as well as the Mahicans east of the Hudson River who were enemies of the Mohawks, in particular. The collective tribes had been raiding and skirmishing with each other for generations, but as Haudenosaunee power began to grow, concerted war did too, especially for the Mohawks living in close proximity to the St. Lawrence Valley. A previous battle in 1603 had resulted in the deaths of over one hundred Mohawks. To celebrate the event, and show to all their people that vengeance had been satisfied for previous transgressions, the victorious Algonquin cut the heads off their dead enemies and prominently displayed them in their villages. [26] Hauling enemy's heads back to villages was a chore, and it was during this time period that cutting off the skin or scalp of the dead enemy's head and retaining it by drying and stretching it on a wooden hoop was initiated. Taking an enemy's scalp once they were killed was more a trophy that an outward display of fulfilled vengeance. "Very good evidence for the assumption that the scalp trophy was a development of the head trophy and that the Indians were originally all head-hunters is afforded by the native pictography. In this the scalped bodies are always represented headless....It is certain that head taking preceded scalp taking and that the latter was a development from the former." [27] Still, cutting off the entire head and displaying it, as the Huron did with the Iroquois victims,

47

had its time and place more so as an act of demonstrating with the evidence that a settling of an old score by taking the guilty party or their associate's life that needed to be done had been accomplished.

What changed the nature of their warfare after 1603 was the introduction of European weaponry to the theatre; in this case, the French and their arquebus, a variation of a matchlock muzzle-loading musket. In the summer of 1609 Samuel de Champlain, recently arrived to the fledgling colony of New France, accompanied a sizable Montagnais, Huron, and Algonquin war party on an expedition to make war upon the Mohawks and their league brothers, whom Champlain called Iroquois. The northern Indian alliance petitioned Champlain and he readily accepted, without comprehending what consequences might occur in taking sides in the age-old Indian dispute. After ascending what Champlain called, "The River of the Iroquois," now known as the Richelieu River, Champlain, his small party of French men, and hundreds of allied Indians met a sizable army of Iroquois on July 29th. A battle ensued the next day near Ticonderoga at the southern end of Lake Champlain. [28] In the brief skirmish that followed the advance of two hundred Iroquois warriors armed with bows and war clubs, Champlain noted in his journal that he and his men fired their black-powder muskets at the center of the Iroquois warriors where three chiefs were spotted. One of Champlain's own musket balls killed two of the Mohawk chiefs outright; a third chief was killed by one of Champlain's men. Having never been exposed to musket fire before, the Iroquois broke and ran after sustaining numerous casualties, whereupon Champlain's Indian allies rushed after the fleeing Iroquois, routing them. The wounded Iroquois warriors left behind on the battlefield were dispatched by the French Indians and twelve captives were taken prisoner, and subsequently roasted alive for entertainment that evening, in celebration of the victory.

Haudenosaunee reprisals against the French-allied Indians followed on a large scale. With an every growing dense population, they were able to field a large number of warriors continuously to attack their traditional enemies, as well as the French in Canada who were now a new, dangerous foe to contend with. The Haudenosaunee were about to live up to the names given to them, "Black Snakes, Killer People, and the Iroquois." From a number of warpaths radiating out of Iroquoia, long lines of Iroquois warriors moving in single file headed northward in the ensuing years. Choosing to carefully avoid again a pitched battle in which the French and their muskets could make them ready targets, the Iroquois warriors shifted their tactics to ambush and war on the run. Revenge was the primary motive, but not the only one. Their enemies allied with the French had access to European goods and weapons that the Iroquois wanted and needed. This access had come about through the fur trade which the French encouraged. While the Iroquois had gained some of the metal wares brought by French missionaries and diplomats, and what was traded for with other Indians, or plundered from them in war, it was not in quantities sufficient. Consequently, the first decade or two of warfare in the north had brought the Iroquois mixed results. The French always held the balance of power with their superior weapons, but that was about to change.

The Dutch expanded their presence in America in 1624 by establishing a trading post at what is now Albany, New York. Seizing the initiative to regain the balance of power in their on-going war with the French and their allies, the Iroquois began trading furs to the

Dutch for metal tools and weapons vital for the survival of their culture. At the same time, with the introduction of metal traps, the Iroquois acquired the means to obtain valuable fur pelts, especially the beaver, which hastened their trade with their new partners, the Dutch. By around 1640, the beaver were trapped to near-extinction in their own lands, so the Iroquois set their sights on conquering the Indians to the north to obtain their fur trade for themselves, which became known as the "Beaver Wars." [29] Another reason for stepping up warfare with the tribes to the north was that the Iroquois needed captives to bolster their lagging populations that had suffered significant losses of warriors on the battlefield, as well as to smallpox and other white-man's diseases which had inadvertently been spread to them by both the French and Dutch. Hundreds had perished during the years of pestilence during the 1630's for which the Iroquois had no immunity. "The full impact of smallpox, measles, and other communicable diseases on Indian populations is notoriously hard to calculate, but historians estimate that over the course of the seventeenth century, the entire Iroquois population was probably halved from about twenty thousand to ten thousand by this onslaught." Revenge, furs, and captives were the reasons the Iroquois picked up the pace of their warfare by the end of the 1630's.

The Iroquois had no other choice than to mount a more aggressive campaign against their enemies. Since the French fur trade had now shifted to the Huron and Neutral Indian nations north of them, the Iroquois who no longer had beaver pelts to trade were unable to obtain the trade goods they needed from the Dutch. In addition, the French with their muskets had inflicted significant losses on the battlefield during the see-saw conflict of the 1630s and early 1640's. Coupled with waves of disease sweeping through Iroquoia, the populations of the Iroquois castles was fast declining, and only the influx of large numbers of adopted captives could change that. What finally reversed these setbacks for the Iroquois came from the Dutch, who were keenly aware that the French were now dominating the fur trade. Eager to checkmate their French rivals to the north and become masters of the fur trade in their own right, "In 1648, the Dutch authorized selling guns directly to the Mohawk rather than through traders, and promptly sold 400 to the Iroquois." [30] The resulting turnaround was stunning. Over a thousand armed warriors attacked Huronia in devastating waves. Major Huron villages were attacked, pillaged and destroyed. The Huron warriors defending them were overrun and annihilated and the remaining population taken captive and brought back to Iroquoia for adoption or death, which numbered in the thousands. Those Huron people able to escape fled westward and soon Huronia was depopulated. The hated Jesuit missionaries captured in the Huron villages were tortured and killed. The Iroquois blamed the priests of bringing deadly disease to their people along with their Christian religion, and the Iroquois were not alone in suspecting the Black Robes were the source of contagion. A French nun in 1640 wrote, "One of the oldest and most prominent women of this [Huron] nation harangued an assembly in this way: 'It is the Black Robes that make us die by their spells. Hearken to me, I am proving by arguments you will know to be true. They lodged in a certain village where everyone was well. As soon as they were established there, everyone was dead except for three or four persons.' " [31]

With the Huron out of the way, the Iroquois turned their full fury against the French who had supported the Huron. Vengeance for past French outrages going back to Champlain was foremost in the minds of the Iroquois warriors. With brutal efficiency,

Iroquois war parties travelled rapidly along Lake Champlain and down the Richelieu River where they split up and began systematically raiding the outlying farms and villages of the St. Lawrence River Valley. Montreal itself was blockaded by the Iroquois. They intercepted fur traders returning from the Great Lakes. A vast amount of furs and goods were taken back to Iroquoia, along with captured women and children for adoption. In May of 1660, Iroquois warriors attacked Montreal, capturing many French captives. In 1661, another force attacked villages near Quebec and netted prisoners again. At the same time, the Iroquois successfully fought a series of battles with the Mahicans Indians east of the Hudson River to gain total access to the fur trade with the Dutch at Fort Orange, later named Albany. When the Mahicans were defeated, the Iroquois set their sights on conquering the Eries, Petuns and Neutral tribes adjacent to the former Huron, on both the north and south sides of Lake Erie. With the Huron defeated in 1649, the Petuns tribe in 1650, and the Neutral nation in 1651, all that remained for the Iroquois to subdue in the immediate Great Lakes region was the Eries living on their lands south of Lake Erie into the Ohio Country.

The Iroquois defeated their ancestral enemies, the Eries, in a series of battles beginning in the mid-1650's that culminated in a direct attack that exterminated them. The Eries were called by the French Jesuits the "Cat People" because of the large number wildcats living in their lands that were "two or three times as large as our tame cats, but having a beautiful and precious fur." [32] Having incurred the wrath of the Iroquois for sheltering Huron refugees from the Iroquois destruction of Huronia in 1649, the Iroquois mobilized a sizable army of warriors and invaded Erie land with the intent of destroying them too. The Eries lived much as the Iroquois to the east of them, in fortified collections of longhouses with palisaded walls surrounding them. Unfortunately for the Eries, their distance from Montreal and the disruption of their fur trade with the French had left them without many musket weapons, forcing them to rely upon less accurate bows and arrows for defense. The Iroquois attacked the main Erie castle and gained entrance by scaling the walls using canoes as ladders, whereupon they slaughtered the entire population, choosing not to adopt most who surrendered. Few escaped, and most captives were roasted by the Iroquois, according to a Jesuit account. [33] As a result the former Erie lands south of the shores of Lake Erie were effectively depopulated by the Iroquois, who now claimed the land as their own with exclusive hunting rights.

At the end of the decade, the Iroquois, flushed with victory, turned their attention to their ancestral enemy, the war-like Susquehannocks tribe to the south, in the lower Susquehanna River Valley. They too, like the Iroquois, had been waging intermittent war against their neighbors for generations, including the Haudenosaunee. Like the Iroquois, the Susquehannocks lived in palisaded towns or castles for protection. Iroquois war parties began moving down the network of warpaths to the south of Iroquois lands through what is now known as central Pennsylvania. In addition to the sizable number of warriors that the Susquehannocks could field, they were allied with the Lenape, or Delaware Indians, as well as the English in their Maryland colony. The English were fearful of Iroquois expansion into Maryland and thought it wise to provide the Susquehannocks with weapons, including light artillery pieces. In 1663, the Iroquois sent an army of over 800 warriors into Susquehannock territory to attack a key palisaded castle, but were repulsed, in part, by

Susquehannock use of the artillery given to them by the English. Undaunted, the Iroquois continued the war for the next eleven years, which see-sawed back and forth, in a series of raids and reprisals with no end. It was only after the English ended their alliance with the Susquehannocks, having seen the need to seek a peace treaty with the Iroquois after the French invaded Iroquoia in 1666 that the tide turned against the Susquehannocks, which led to their defeat in 1677, by a combined Iroquois and English army. The Iroquois claimed all Susquehannock lands as their own and the English acknowledged the Iroquois claim.

By 1660, the Haudenosaunee League had reached their zenith of power and conquest. However, they were unable to sustain it. Continual, costly wars had depleted them of warriors and resources for a second time. In spite of the adoption of hundreds of enemy captives to bolster their population, and the acquisition of plunder and foodstuffs from the conquered lands to support their own warriors in the field, simply, the Haudenosaunee were depleted. As if sensing the moment had come to retaliate in kind, the French in Canada decided that an invasion of Iroquoia was long overdue in order to punish them Iroquois for their transgressions. Their reasons for retribution were long, especially against the Mohawks. The Iroquois had undone all the good that the French had brought with them for New France to survive and prosper. The French fur trade with the own Indian allies was irreparably damaged from the attacks of the Iroquois into the French sphere of influence. In addition, the Hurons, who served the French as a buffer between Iroquoia and New France had been effectively destroyed, and the Eries, with their furs, wiped out of existence. Further, the Jesuit mission to bring Christianity to the Indians had been seriously set back with the martyred deaths of eight Black Robes at the hands of the Iroquois. Finally, the security and peace of mind of the French citizens of New France had been shattered by the Iroquois attacks into Canada. The growth and prosperity of the colony had been jeopardized to the point that something had to be done with the Iroquois question to reverse the dire situation.

That decision to punish the Iroquois came from France itself. A new governor, Baron du Bois d'Avaugour was sent to Canada in 1661 "to plant Lilies over the ashes of the Iroquois," as quoted by a Jesuit priest in New France. [34] Following the new governor were a contingent of regular French soldiers from the Carignan-Salieres Regiment sent to Canada to beef up the militia there. A winter military campaign was planned for January of 1666. A significant French and allied Indian force of more than four hundred combined men left Montreal for the Mohawk villages. They never made it there due to the extreme cold and snowy cold conditions, and turned back after reaching the outskirts of the little Dutch town of Schenectady on the Mohawk River. Undaunted, the French massed an army of regular troops, militia and allied Indians for a second campaign in 1666, this time under the command of the Marquis de Tracy. Arriving at the first Mohawk village on October 15th they French found the fortified castle recently abandoned. The Mohawks fled rather than fight, giving the French the opportunity to burn and pillage the longhouses and surrounding fields before pursuing the Mohawks to their next castle. Three other Mohawk castles in succession were attacked by the French and found undefended. Storehouses full of corn and provisions were destroyed. At the last castle, the French, "were hopeful of meeting with a stout resistance, which they prepared to attack in regular form....but our men were again disappointed in their hope; for scarcely had the enemy seen the advance-guard approaching, when they promptly took flight to the woods," recorded a Jesuit priest who accompanied the French army. [35] Having struck a great blow against the Iroquois, and the Mohawks in particular, de Tracy and his army returned victorious to Canada. Promptly the Iroquois sued for peace with the French, which was accepted.

Now at peace with the French, the Iroquois were free to continue their war on a much smaller scale with the Susquehannocks, as well as the scattered tribes of the Ohio Country. A significant change had come to the Iroquois' trading partners at Fort Orange. In 1664, the British invaded the Dutch possession of New Amsterdam at the mouth of the Hudson River, and forced the Dutch to surrender the city, which the English re-named New York, and claimed all the Dutch possessions in the colony of New Netherland as their own. Within a year, the English occupied the village of Fort Orange on the Hudson River at the mouth of the Mohawk River, and assumed control of the former Dutch fur trade. Overnight, the Iroquois had a new trading partner, the English. By 1667, a formal agreement was reached between the Iroquois and the English they both called the "Covenant Chain," with Albany designated as the site for the formal council fire for all future English-Iroquois agreements. [36] Councils between them were opened with a ritual called the "condolence ceremony," a throwback to the early formation of the Haudenosaunee League. "Each side took a turn as the 'clear-minded' moiety, giving three strings of the marine shell beads known as wampum to the other side to assuage their grief and clear their eye, ears, and throat, so that they might see, hear, and speak clearly again. The bulk of the proceedings were then given over to speeches, as each side presented and responded to grievances and requests concerning trade, land, and alliances." [37]

The firm, unwavering treaty with the English sealed the fate of the Susquehannocks of the lower Susquehanna River Valley. The English supplied the Iroquois with arms and ammunition to continue their war. The Susquehannocks, who once were able to field many fierce warriors were now reduced to shadow of their former greatness, and were unable to successfully defend themselves from concerted Iroquois aggression. The Iroquois defeated them in a number of battles and absorbed the survivors or killed them. To the far west in the Ohio Country now depopulated of the Eries in the north, the Iroquois finished their conquest of the lands drained by the Ohio River by expelling several minor Siouan-speaking tribes residing there. Some Shawnee living in the Ohio Country above the Ohio River were attacked and driven west as refugees to the powerful Miami Indian tribe who resisted Iroquois expansion for all while before fleeing west themselves after Iroquois warriors attacked and destroyed a Miami village. Iroquois war parties ranged as far west as the Illinois Country and as far south as Tennessee and Virginia in the continued quest to consolidate land acquisitions through war. However, with Iroquois manpower declining, and no way to populate the Ohio Country permanently, the Iroquois were going to have to settle for keeping the conquered lands as exclusive hunting and trapping domains by continued military means. So it came as no wonder that La Salle, in his expedition down the Ohio River in 1669, found the Ohio Country an empty country, devoid of native people who had once lived there. The Ohio Country now belonged to the Iroquois and under their jurisdiction, with the constant threat that interlopers wishing to trespass to hunt risked the wrath of the new owners to the far northeast.

Place of the Skull

Chapter 4: The First White Traders

As the lands of the Ohio Country lay empty near the turn of the century, that was not the case east of the Allegheny Mountains in the great Susquehanna and Delaware River valleys that had once been the home of the Susquehannocks. With the hostile Indians gone by and large by 1700, William Penn's colony began to expand north and west from Philadelphia, acquiring land parcels from the Delaware Indians who had been quietly migrating into former Susquehannock lands along the east side of the Susquehanna River and northward from their former homes on the lower Delaware River. Land along that river was gobbled up by English expansion. By 1718, all of the Delaware formerly living there were gone westward to the Susquehanna. In the Ohio Country, with Iroquois authority all but non-existent, the Miami Indians who had fled westward toward the Illinois Country gradually returned to their former lands along the Miami River. Some of the Shawnee who had inhabited parts of the Ohio Country in the mid-1600's and moved to the Mississippi Valley below the mouth of the Ohio during the wars with the Iroquois, made their way back to Ohio lands. In all cases, while the Iroquois were aware of these incursions into their hunting lands, they did not go to war over it. Peace had been momentarily restored to the region of the Ohio Country only because the Iroquois no longer had the means to expel interlopers by force, as they had once done in the past. In fact, Shawnee clans migrated from the Potomac and Cumberland valleys to the lands of Pennsylvania to be close to English trade goods which were cheaper and more plentiful than French far to the north of the Ohio Country. Again, the Iroquois did not directly interfere.

The Iroquois acquiesced in the Ohio Country because they could not create, nor keep a permanent presence everywhere. Rather, beginning in the 1690's, Iroquois families from primarily the Seneca began to migrate southward, setting up hunting camps, and then small villages on a more permanent basis. They used the waterways of the upper reaches of the Allegheny River to travel to new homes. This gradual migration of Iroquois included people from all the united tribes, but least the Mohawks in the east of the confederacy. The upper reaches of the Susquehanna River and its large network of tributaries were equally used for the Iroquois migration southward into Pennsylvania, all the while reminding their English allies in the southeast Philadelphia region of the mutual agreements made in the past that allowed for Iroquois possession of the lands they claimed by conquest. The move southward was not a landslide of Iroquois people but a trickle over a couple of generations. The harsh reality for the Onondaga Council of the League was that their former dominance of all the regions surrounding them was waning. The French to the north were becoming a more immediate threat to Iroquois security, as they became more and more embroiled in the conflict with the expanding English colonies over land and sovereignty. The lightning strike by a French military force of 250 men, including French-allied Indians in January of 1704 against the town of Deerfield, Massachusetts shook Iroquois confidence as to ultimate French intentions. Would they be attacked next in the conflict known in America as Queen Anne's War?

The fact of the matter was that the Iroquois had little manpower to establish anything permanent in the Ohio Country beyond small villages and camps along creeks and rivers that were accessible by canoe, as well as the major war paths and trails that radiated southward from Seneca land that was used in previous wars. The Iroquois understood that the best they could do was to migrate on a smaller scale and create a minimal presence with the resources available. By doing so, they could exert some control over the other tribes immigrating to the region, who were both sympathetic to the English as allies and united with the Iroquois in their enduring hatred of the Indian enemies to the south. The Catawba and Cherokee were attempting to make inroads into the Iroquois lands to the south of the Ohio River, in Kentucky and the Kanawha River valley. Consequently, by 1720, Iroquois villages of 10-20 families in a several dozen cabins and wigwams had sprung up on the west side of the Alleghenies along the upper reaches of the Allegheny River. Connewango, Buckaloon, Yoghroonwago and Jenuchshadego were small Iroquois villages on the upper Allegheny that came into existence, populated by a mix of Seneca, Cayuga and Oneida families, with in some cases, a smattering of other tribes like Delaware, such as that found at Buckaloon, named in English, Broken Straw. [38] The village of Maghinquechahocking, situated about 20 miles above Venango on French Creek, a tributary of the Allegheny founded at the same time as Iroquois villages in the area was primarily Shawnee with a mix of Delaware and Iroquois. [39] This indicated that the Shawnee migration from the Maryland area that began in 1694 was now reaching the Ohio Country, as they travelled from the Potomac north on the old Warrior's Trail and Catawba Path that Iroquois war parties used to attack their southern enemies.

Further Iroquois expansion into the Ohio Country continued into the early 1720's but it was not exclusively Iroquois any longer. While similar-sized Iroquois villages sprouted up in what is now northern Pennsylvania along the upper reaches of the Susquehanna River, the English were expanding westward into the lower Susquehanna Valley, squeezing the Delaware into ever decreasing places of their own east of the river. English settlers were flooding into former Indian lands that were sold from under them by the Iroquois themselves who maintained that the Delaware had no rights to the land that the Iroquois had conquered and lay claim to. By 1723, many Delaware and Shawnee living east of the Susquehanna began heading west, across the Allegheny Mountains to settle in the Ohio Country. As a result, mixed Iroquois, Delaware, and Shawnee migrants found themselves reaching the Ohio River Valley and establishing villages. Kittanning, on the Allegheny River above the Forks of the Ohio was the largest of these new multi-tribe settlements, which was largely Delaware in makeup. Kittanning, meaning "At the Great River," afforded some fifty families and more than 150 men. "There were several villages along the river front at this place, scattered along both sides of the river. The term 'Allegheny on the Main Road,' which is frequently used in the early records, no doubt had reference to this place, as well as others, on the 'main road' of the Iroquois along the Allegheny River. This was the chief war path of the Iroquois to the Mississippi, and had been used by the Senecas in their war expeditions for many years before the coming of the Delaware and Shawnee to the region. In the 'Memoir' of 1718, it is stated that 'The River Ohio is the route which the Iroquois take." [40]

Downriver from the major village of Kittanning was Shannopin's Town, about two miles north of the Forks of the Ohio on the east bank of the Allegheny River. It too was primarily a Delaware village though it had Indians of many tribes living there. The village was named after the Delaware Chief Shannopin, and became a prominent gathering place for Indians as well as French and English traders visiting the town in the

1720's. Shannopin's Town lay at the end of a major east-west Indian trail that crossed the Allegheny Mountains and connected with the Indian paths of the Susquehanna River Valley, being approximately 230 miles from the river itself. The ancient trail that wound its way through the mountains from the Susquehanna to the Ohio Rivers became known as, "The Raystown Path," named after an early English trader and explorer named John Wray. [41] At Shannopin's town on the Ohio, the trail forded the shallows and headed west. "At Shannopin's there is a fording place in very dry times and the lowest down the river," it was reported. [42] Below Shannopin's lay the major Indian village that would come to be known by the English as Logstown, about 18 miles below the Forks, on the north bank of the Ohio. Logstown was multi-tribal as well, established around 1725. It was inhabited primarily by Delaware, Shawnee, and Iroquois Seneca, with "a few Wyandot [Huron,] Mohawk and Miami living in the settlement at various times." [43] Logstown, too, lay on the main Iroquois war paths that ran southwest down the Ohio River and a spur running west into the heart of the Ohio Country. A few miles below Logstown on the same side of the Ohio along the Iroquois trail was another Indian village below the mouth of the Beaver River that emptied into the Ohio. The village became known as King Beaver's Town or Shingas Town after the Delaware brothers Tamaque or "King Beaver" and Shingas, who were Delaware chiefs. The village was a mix of Delaware, Shawnee and Iroquois families, situated at the juncture of a trail that headed up the Beaver River to the Great Lakes region and that of the Iroquois trail following the Ohio both up and down river. Consequently the village was a crossroads for not only Indians but white traders to the Indians from all over the Ohio Country for years to come.

Below the village of Beaver were a number of small villages and hunting camps on both sides of the Ohio, usually located at the mouths of creeks and streams flowing into it. Said a French trader reporting to the Pennsylvania Council by letter on the Indians in hunting camps along the Ohio River, "The number of Indians who have settled on this river increases every day. Ammunition is very scarce at this time, when deer hunting begins. There have come from afar some Indians loaded with peltries, in order to buy powder [gunpowder.] [44] A group of Oneida Iroquois families settled at the mouth of Yellow Creek on the west side of the Ohio above what is now the city of Steubenville. The Oneida chief Shickellamy, who lived in a village on the west branch of the Susquehanna River, had a son named Taghneghdorus, otherwise called John Shickellamy, and later known simply as Logan. Logan's mother was a Cayuga, and as such, Logan inherited his Iroquois lineage and status through her, and not his father. Logan became one of ten Cayuga sachems or council chiefs of the Iroquois, and later moved with his family from Pennsylvania to Yellow Creek on the Ohio. Logan would become known in the Ohio Country, not as a Cayuga Indian, but by a new word given to all Iroquois living in the Ohio Country who had migrated there. The Delaware name for the Iroquois came from the Algonquin language which meant "stealthy and treacherous." [45] The word "Mengwe" or "Minquas" was originally used by the Delaware to describe all tribes of Iroquoian descent, including Susquehannocks. Later, the word was corrupted by the English into the word "Mingo" which was used to identify Indians in the Ohio Country who were of Iroquois bloodline. [46]

By the early 1700's, wherever the Indians migrated, English traders soon followed. It is recorded that the first white man to travel down the Allegheny and

Ohio River after La Salle was a Dutch trader from Albany on the Hudson River named Arent or Arnold Viele. Viele was known to be an Iroquois interpreter who attended the councils of the Iroquois at Onondaga as a representative of the New York colony government. Viele was said to have lived among the Indians for years, and travelled extensively, visiting the Ohio Country in 1694 in the company of Shawnee and Iroquois. [47] An exact date of the first Englishman to cross the Alleghenies and see the Ohio River for the first time is unknown. It is generally believed that the very first explorer turned trader, James Le Tort, arrived along the old Indian trails prior to 1720, and as early as 1717. [48] Records show that LeTort's father was, "A French Hugenot who came to America in 1686, from London. In 1693 he and his wife, Anne, were engaged in the Indian trade at Schuylkill. He began his Indian trade at Conestoga about 1695." [49] Le Tort's son, James, worked with his father in the trading business, and applied for his own license to trade with the Indians in 1713. In 1719, he settled on the east side of Susquehanna River near Conestoga to better serve his trading business with the Shawnee, who were said to have emigrated to the Susquehanna Valley from 1692-1694 from Maryland. [50] Sometime thereabouts, Le Tort accompanied the Indians across the path from the Susquehanna to the Allegheny River called the Allegheny Path, the Ohio Path, and much later, the Frankstown Path. [51] It is believed that in those early years, Le Tort travelled down the Ohio River all the way to the Miami Indians on the Wabash, trading English goods with all Indians for their furs. After establishing his trading business with the Ohio Indians, LeTort moved across the Susquehanna into Iroquois territory to a place he called Le Tort's Spring just east of the mountains. Here he built a trading post which later would become the village of Carlisle.

Another early explorer and trader who crossed the Allegheny Mountains was Peter Bezaillion, a friend of James Le Tort. Bezaillion, older than Le Tort, may have been a French Hugenot who accompanied the senior Le Tort. In 1710, according to Pennsylvania records, Bezaillion was trading with the Indians near Conestoga, and was licensed by the colony in 1712. He acted as an interpreter for the colony at a council held with the Indians at Conestoga on July 18, 1717. Bezaillion's wife's brother, Moses Coombe, was likewise a trader, and it is likely that Le Tort, Bezaillion and Coombe travelled across the mountains on many occasions to trade with the Ohio Indians. A third Frenchman, a French Canadian named Martin Chartier, was known to have "led the Shawnee from the west and south to the head of Chesapeake Bay in 1692." [52] Martin Chartier married a Shawnee Indian and carried on a trade with them on the Susquehanna. His only son, Peter, followed in his father's footsteps, engaging in the fur trade with the Shawnee, and marrying a Shawnee woman. Like Le Tort, Chartier moved to the west side of the Susquehanna and began making trips across the mountains to the Ohio Country. When the Turtle and Turkey clans of the Delaware Indians began to move across the mountains to the Allegheny River beginning in 1724, Chartier followed. Soon after, Chartier was counseling the Shawnee living east of the Alleghenies to likewise move west to the Ohio Country.

There were early other traders to the Indians. John Harris Sr. came to America in 1698 from Yorkshire, England, and moved from Philadelphia to the Conestoga area some time before 1718, to engage in trade with the Indians there. [53] Later, Harris moved north and built a trading house on the Susquehanna River, and founded a ferry service across the river when it was too high to travel across the shallow ford. In 1734, he applied to "build a small house on the west side of the said River for the convenience of Travellers that may happen to come on that side in the Night Season or in Stormy Weather when the Boat or Flat cannot pass." [54] Harris's petition was granted by Philadelphia authorities but the Iroquois, who laid claim to the land west of the river, objected. The Iroquois chief Shikellamy complained to Provincial authorities for Harris to "desist from making a plantation…where Harris has built a House and is clearing fields," whereupon he was told that Harris "only built his house for carrying on his trade." Shikellamy replied, "That though Harris may have built a House for the conveniency of his trade, yet he ought not to clear fields." [55] Clearly the Iroquois were beginning to feel the pressure of white settlement west of the Susquehanna River up to the Allegheny Mountains which they forbid, but were powerless to stop. Harris soon built a thriving trade and ferry business as a main stopping point for anyone heading west into the mountains. Harris would go on to build barns to store trade goods and furs, and compute mileages from his place to stopping points along the Allegheny Path.

Edmund Cartlidge was another early trader to cross the mountains to the Ohio Country. Edmund and his brother John, who were Quakers from Philadelphia, began trading in the east as early as 1702. In 1716, both brothers petitioned the government for warrants of land in the Conestoga area to further their trade with the Indians. On a trading trip in 1722 at a Seneca hunting camp in northern Maryland, a drunken Indian attacked John Cartlidge after he refused to give him any more rum. Cartlidge killed the Indian, and both brothers were jailed until the Iroquois intervened and got them released. Edmund, who became licensed, travelled across the mountains to the Ohio Country numerous times after the death of his brother in 1726. [56] Other licensed traders were soon to follow in the early footsteps of Cartlidge, Harris, Bezaillion, Chartier, and Le Tort. Lazarus, James, and Alexander Lowry became licensed traders, as well as Jonas Davenport, Thomas Perrin, James Patterson, John Lawrence, Patrick Boyd, Peter Allen, and Frank Stevens. Recorded petitions of 1730 in Philadelphia list them by name, and indicate that some of them claimed to have begun trading thirteen years ago, in 1717. [57] Soon too many men to count became involved in the Indian trade business of hauling goods across the Allegheny Mountains to the Ohio Indians and beyond. Unspoken in all this was the shocking number of unlicensed traders hot on the heels of the licensed traders, bringing illegal goods to the Indians for high profits. The terrible pernicious rum trade that would debauch Indians everywhere and strip them of all their possessions was in full swing, hot on the heels of legitimate traders.

What Indians everywhere on the frontier and beyond needed most was all kinds of white man's manufactured goods, especially muskets to hunt with, and lead ball and gunpowder to arm themselves with. By 1720, the need to hunt animals was far more important than simply bringing home food to eat. With the all but extinction of the beaver, the fur trade destined for Europe turned to deer and elk skins, and for Indians to kill enough of these game animals for their hides to acquire traders goods in return, they needed weapons that were efficient and deadlier than bows and arrows. When not at war, a great deal of an Indian warrior's time was spent in the woods hunting, either collectively with others where the profits would be equally divided, or alone. Game might be plentiful in the woods from time to time, but not all hunting trips resulted in kills. The animals, once downed, needed skinned, and the meat dressed and then packed for hauling back to camp. Often a warrior took his extended family to the temporary camps. There, the women could dress the animal hides by the backbreaking work of scraping off the meat, fat, and ligament from the skin with knives, so that the process of tanning the hide could begin, if need be. Meat was usually dried and smoked on wooden racks or over fires and then packed for the trip home. Deerskins became the staple of commerce between the Indians and traders with other fur-bearing animals included when available. All in all, procuring, processing, and delivering deerskins was a laborious task, and one deerskin did not buy a great deal of goods, even at English prices which were considerably lower than French.

Other goods of importance to the Indians besides guns and ammunition were everything made from iron, beginning with hatchets, axes and hammers. Pots or all sizes to cook in were valued items every Indian family needed, along with nails, chain, and barrel hoops. Clothing and fabric was a necessary trade item and included colonial shirts, Indian match coats, wool blankets, stroud, and yard goods, and all the things needed to sew with, from thread to iron needles. Personal items were popular, and included mirrors, beads, ribbon, medallions, trinkets, silver earrings, brooches, and vermillion paint. The trader, fluent in the native language, set the prices and kept a detailed ledger of all transactions, and with whom. He usually planned his appearance at the Indian villages in summer before hunting season began when the animal fur was thickening in preparation for the coming winter. Without skins yet to trade, the trader offered the Indian customers he knew and dealt with credit upon which he would collect in the late spring when he returned, whereupon the debt would be paid in full. That way the trader could return over the mountains to the east with the furs and skins, and pay off his own debt to his suppliers in Philadelphia who had fronted him the goods in the first place. Everything hinged on the trader making the trips on time, and on the Indians having been successful at hunting and dressing the hides. Once the haggling over prices was completed and the goods and animal skins transferred to the trader's own men to pack, traders were expected to treat their Indian trading partners to liquor, usually rum, to celebrate the occasion.

Traders found it was more efficient and profitable to bring the trade goods to the Indians along the Ohio River than for the Indians to traverse the mountains to the east. One reason was the general lack of horses available to the Indians, which meant that they could not haul a large quantity of furs across the trails nor buy a lot when they did do so. Traders were able to tie a large load of goods on specially-made racks for the backs of horses. A trader could navigate the mountain trails that were large enough to allow for a horse to pass, but profitability meant that he had to bring six or more goods-laden horses with him on each trip. Unable to handle a number of horses alone during the two-week trip or longer, the trader usually hired 3-4 men to work for him. They were required to keep the horses together in a line during the daily travel, and when stopping to rest or camp for the night, the employees unsaddled the horses, and made sure that they were fed, watered, and hobbled for the night. There was always a risk the horses would wander off looking for scarce forage on their own. It took only a trip or two for a trader's men to become acquainted with the Indian path, its landmarks, watering holes or springs, its foraging fields, and the most secure stopping points. Employees were armed with muskets for protection from wild predators such as wolves, mountain lions, and bears. And one never knew when they might be attacked by thieves, Indians, or other traders once they were far from civilization in the mountain wilderness where the only protection was what one could provide for himself.

Place of the Skull

Chapter 5: The Rum Runners

It didn't take long for trouble to arise west of the Alleghenies over liquor and unlicensed traders. Every white man trading with the Indians both east and west of the mountains knew the well-known fact that Indians couldn't hold their liquor. Traders had discovered long ago what the people in Philadelphia suspected; that all Indians had a natural weakness for alcohol, and it didn't take a whole lot of it in any form for them to get senseless drunk, unlike a white man. Not only was it a weakness of their physical nature that they easily became drunk, but an addiction for liquor for which they had absolutely no defense. While drunk, Indians were liable to do anything imaginable. Often, while in drunken states from white man's rum and whiskey, Indians would get involved in rip-roaring fights with each other that resulted in grave injuries, and even death, to which they had no recollection the next day upon sobering up. It was a weakness that unscrupulous traders immediately began to take advantage of. Rum consumption would drive Indians crazy, and yet they always wanted more. Conrad Weiser, adopted son of the Iroquois, lived among them for years in the early part of the 18th century. Weiser went on to become Pennsylvania's Indian ambassador for the rest of his life because he knew Indian nature, culture and personality intimately. He commented on the introduction of rum traders. "One can be among them [Indians] for thirty years and more, and never once see two sober Indians fight and quarrel except when drunk on rum obtained from rum traders." [58]

Typically, their weakness for liquor caused havoc among all the Indian tribes. Drunken Indians had stolen, knifed, tomahawked, shot, and thrown each other into fires without any restraint. A letter written at

Shannopin's Town on the Ohio, by either Cartlidge or Le Tort, and signed with the mark of Shannopin, the Delaware chief himself, explained the death of the trader John Hart. Hart had been killed "in a drunken fight at Shannopin's Town in the fall of 1729." Another trader, David Robeson had been wounded by a drunken Shawnee woman, all due to the drunken Indian brawls resulting from the unrestricted sale of rum to the Indians. When Indians ran out of liquor, they would lie, steal, and cheat to get more due to their addiction. Weiser was acutely aware of the effects of liquor upon the Indians and how it affected his deliberations with them, depending upon their state of inebriation or sobriety. Writing about a particular Indian, Conrad noted, "I bought two quarts of Rum there [at John Harris trading post] to use on our Journey but he [the Indian] drunk most of it the first day. He abused me very much Cursed and Swore and asked pardon when he got Sober. Did the same again when he was drunk again. Damned me more than hundred times, so he did the Governor and Mr. Peters for not paying him for his trouble and Expenses, he is vexed at the new purchase told me I Cheated the Indians, he Says he will now Kill any white men that will pretend to settle on his Creek, and that the Governor and Mr. Peters told him So much Saying he was a warrior, how he could suffer the Irish to encroach upon him he would now act according to advice and kill some of them. I reprimanded him when sober, he begged pardon, desired me not to mention it to you, but did the same again at another drunken frolic. I left him drunk at Achwick, on one leg he had a Stocking and no Shoe, on the other a Shoe and no Stocking." [59] Summing up the deplorable situation he often found himself in when trying to deal with drunken Indians, Weiser noted, "When they [Indians] wanted more Rum, they would frequently complain and say they had been cheated;

which will be the case always as long as there are any Indians, and as long as they can get Rum." [60]

Clearly, the Indians became dangerous to themselves and others when drinking. This danger [61] caused licensed traders to carry conservative amounts of liquor across the mountains, and use extreme caution in allowing Indians to purchase rum from them which could easily jeopardize their own lives and that of their skin purchases, if the Indians became drunk. But this situation was nothing new for the frontier between whites and Indians. Traders had been plying their alcohol wares to Indians since the beginning of trade between them and dated back to the 1600's when the Dutch brought alcohol to the Iroquois in copious amounts. Liquor, especially rum, was both plentiful and cheap. Sugar and molasses was a staple imported from the Caribbean Islands, as one leg of the triangle of trade involving English manufactured goods and African slaves. In the colonies of Pennsylvania and New England, molasses was easily distilled into rum for domestic consumption, for the trading with the Indians, and for export to Europe. The provincial government of Pennsylvania addressed the growing rum problem with Indians as early as 1700. In recognition of the number of illicit rum traders, they passed a law requiring that all unlicensed traders be arrested by justices of the peace. The problem was that the law "could not have any effect where there were no justices of the peace," as in the wilderness. [62] Keeping unscrupulous, unlicensed traders out of the Ohio Country and elsewhere was proving impossible for the Quaker government to enforce with a law that had no teeth. Some whispered that there were Quakers in the government that had a personal interest in the rum business and were quietly making huge profits on the side, while mouthing that the rum trade with the Indians must be somehow stopped.

The rum traders to the Ohio Country were most often former employees of licensed traders who had worked for people like Le Tort, Bezaillion, Chartier, Cartlidge and others for a short period of time before embarking upon their own trade. In the course of a trip or two across the mountains, they came to learn the landmarks, turn-offs and resting places of the Allegheny Path. Going out on their own was the next logical step, except they didn't intend on starting a legitimate business. All eyes had witnessed the Indian weakness for liquor. Once an Indian had a taste of it, he went crazy, and would trade everything he possessed, even the clothes off his back and his wife, to get more liquor. This meant that an unscrupulous trader could bring mostly rum to the Indians and hastily depart with all the furs and skins they possessed while the Indians were drunk. Recognizing the problem, as early as 1722 Pennsylvania passed a law entitled, "An Act to prohibit the selling of Rum and other Strong Liquors to the Indians, and to prevent the Abuses that may happen thereby." [63] The law had no effect because rum was plentiful and relatively cheap to buy by the keg in Philadelphia from the right people. The profits were enormous; more than selling the Indians guns, clothing and goods, and it was making fortunes for both the traders and the suppliers. And if that were not enough, the rum traders cleverly planned their trip across the mountains to the Ohio Country early in the spring before the legitimate traders arrived. The licensed traders were shocked to find that the Indians, upon sobering up, discovered that they had no furs to pay off their debts from the previous fall. In addition to being cheated out of their property, they had no credit; thus no means of purchasing guns and ammunition for the fall hunt.

In 1727, the Iroquois themselves petitioned then Governor Patrick Gordon of Pennsylvania to stop the rum traders from entering their lands. They asked that "None of the Traders be allowed to carry any rum to the remoter Parts where James Le Tort trades (that is Allegany on the Branches of the Ohio)." [64] The Iroquois were aware of the debauching effect of liquor upon their people. When they were able to be the middlemen with the Dutch and then the English in the 1600's they controlled how much liquor was brought to their villages. However, all that had changed in the Ohio Country now that traders were going directly to the Indians living on Iroquois lands, and the Iroquois had no means to stop them. By 1730, the illegal rum trade had got completely out of hand. Groups of licensed traders petitioned Governor Gordon directly in Philadelphia, claiming that former employees of theirs were now ruining their trading business. Cartlidge and Davenport complained "that 'Such as had been your petitioners Servants' were making it impossible for the Indians to pay their debts. These undesirable traders would meet the Indians in the spring before Davenport and his associates appeared and with 'a Small parcel of Goods and Large quantityes of Rum' deprive the red men of all their peltry." [65] The result was that the Indians were indebted to Cartlidge and Davenport for two thousand pounds sterling, which they could not collect. Some Indians too, were becoming rum traders themselves. A licensed trader, John Maddox claimed that "certain irresponsible Iroquois Indians in June 1729 had brought fourteen kegs of rum from Albany and sold it to the Delawares on the Allegheny for all the furs that were in their possession." [66] Maddox had been beat and wounded by the Delaware when he refused to give them more goods on credit.

Gordon refused to address the rum problem by controlling the flow of rum from Philadelphia. Instead, he laid down rules and injunctions on October 4, 1729, much like the laws already on the books which stated, "That, as it is prohibited by a Law provided for that purpose, to furnish the Indians with Rum and other Strong Liquors, from the excessive use of which Disorders have frequently ensued, You are carefully to avoid that pernicious Practice." Then, writing a letter directly to the Indians in the Ohio Country who were the victims of the rum trade, Gordon wrote on May 27, 1730, "I therefore order all the Traders that when you have finished your hunting and return with your Skins to your families, those you pay your Skins to shall give you Some Drink to chear you, but at other times you should forbear it." [67] This was more than an admission on the part of the Governor and Pennsylvania authorities that they were not only powerless to stop the illegal rum trade, but implicitly did not want to stop it. Consequently, Gordon was, in effect, telling the Indians to police the illegal rum trade on their own by breaking all rum kegs that were brought into their country. Gordon had had to have known that such a dictum could result in mayhem and murder if the Indians carried it out. Implicit in telling the Indians to stop the trading of rum on their own was the understanding of those in power in Pennsylvania, that the Indians would not be able to stop it on the own. And so the rum trade would continue. Those in government, who might have a hand in seeing the rum trade flourish, would not see their own profits jeopardized. Since the rum traders were always armed as a caution against losing their investment, the failure on the part of the Pennsylvania government was going to ensure that matters with the Ohio Country Indians were going to go from bad to worse. Rum was going to continue to flow westward carried by a swarm of unstoppable liquor traders who would fight to keep their business viable.

In the Ohio Country, the situation deteriorated, as Indian villages were stripped of nearly all their material possessions to trade for liquor. Indians were being cheated as a matter of course, with rum as the medium, which they could not resist. By 1733, the Shawnee living at Chartier's Town had had enough. Four of their chiefs dictated a letter to Governor Gordon seeking the authority to take matters into their own hands, as Gordon had previously advised. "Dear Friends, There is yearly and monthly some new Upstart of a Trader without License who comes amongst Us and brings with him nothing but Rum...but takes away with him those Skins which the old licensed Traders who bring us everything necessary ought to have in Return for their goods sold to us some years since. We therefore beg thou would take it into Consideration and send Us two firm Orders, one for Peter Chartier, the other for Us to break in pieces all the Kegs so brought, and by that Means the old Traders will have their Debts which otherwise never will be paid." [68] With no authorization from the Pennsylvania governor forthcoming, the Indians went one step further and drew up a list of desirable and undesirable traders, informing all that whenever they "saw undesirable traders, they would stave in their Kegs and seize their goods. Each trader must bring his license with him and bring all his Rum to his cabin where he lives directly, and not hide any in the woods. Furthermore, it was provided also that no hired man in the employ of any trader could bring rum into the woods either." [69] The Shawnee news was chilling. Rum traders were put on notice.

Who were these unsavory, underhanded rum runners who would stop at nothing, including the beating and murder of Indians? The Pennsylvania authorities were reluctant to name them for fear that the names of their Philadelphia suppliers might be exposed upon examining them. They were shady people who were well-known to the licensed traders and Indians alike but, by and large, remained unnamed in the council minutes. Rumors circulated that John Harris and his son were involved in the illegal rum trade too, having rum disguised as goods shipped to them at Paxtang on the east side of the Susquehanna River and then once in their possession, hidden in out-buildings away from prying eyes, and loaded on rum traders' horses at night. However, the Shawnee did name some of them, in a letter of protest on April 23, 1733 to the Pennsylvania Governor and Council of Pennsylvania, when other white men would not, or could not. "My Brethren, Sometime ago Edmund (Cartlidge) brought a letter amongst us, and advised me to mind and be careful of my people, and if we wanted any assistance, we might expect it from you; which we are very glad to hear. Edward Kenny, Jacob Pyatt, Timothy Fitzpatrick, William Dunlap and Jonathan Kelly of Donegal, come trading with us without license, which is a hindrance to ye licensed traders. Charles Poke and Thomas Hill are very pernicious, for they have abused us. And at a drinking bout, Henry Bayley, Oliver Wallis, and Jonathan Young, took one of our old men, and after having tied him, abused him very much. James Dunning was among them, and abused us likewise. Such people, we think, are not proper to deal with us. Jonathan Kelly of Paxtang has made a great disturbance by raising false reports among us; and Timothy Fitzpatrick, Thomas Moran, and Jonathan Palmer quarrel often with us; therefore we desire those four men may be kept particularly away." [70] The Shawnee knew from their behavior what vile sort of men the traders were, telling a white man visiting them, "They said, (which I believe is an unhappy and reproachful truth) that they [the traders] would lie, cheat, and debauch their women, and even their wives, if their husband were not at home." [71]

James Dunning's name would appear again in the records of the Pennsylvania council. A Delaware Indian would make allegations against Dunning for robbing him in the Ohio Country sometime in 1746. According to Conrad Weiser who interviewed the Indian and made a report, "Dunning is accused to have stolen forty-seven deer skins and the three horses or mares. The circumstances are very strong. The Indian from whom the skins and horses have been stolen is a Delaware Indian, a sober, quiet, and good-natured man. James Dunning is gone down the Ohio River. The Indian was content that I should inform the Council of his misfortune. He not only lost his skins and horses, but pursued Dunning in vain." [72] What Weiser did not say were the circumstances surrounding the alleged theft. Had Dunning absconded with the Indians horses and furs after trading rum to him and getting him drunk? Sobering up the next day and coming to his senses, the Indian pursued Dunning in an attempt to get his property back that he had been cheated out of. On a different occasion, Dunning complained that he had been robbed of his skins and furs at gunpoint by Peter Chartier and a large party of Shawnee who pursued Dunning when was returning up the Allegheny River in a canoe, in all likelihood, to get to Kittanning, and the trailhead to the Allegheny Path and to the East. [73] Had Dunning, who had a reputation among the Shawnee that caused him to be banned from trading with them, been trading rum to Indians and cheated them out of their furs, and then was caught? Obviously, Peter Chartier was taking the law into his own hands in a lawless land, and Dunning, considered wicked by the Indians, was fortunate that his rum trading deals did not cost him his life.

To strengthen Shawnee resolve over the ruinous situation brought about by the rum traders, Peter Chartier at Chartier's Shawnee Town had a hand in convincing the Shawnee that the real solution to the problem of the illegal rum traders was that the Shawnee take steps to curb their own appetite for rum, if the Delaware and Mingo would not, or could not. A council was held in the winter at Chartier's Town whereupon the Shawnee decided to "Leave off Drinking of Rum for the Space of four years," they informed Governor Gordon. [74] The licensed traders naturally agreed at Chartier's urging. A grand ceremony was held there on March 15, 1738. Then all the rum that "was in the Town was all staved and spilt, belonging to the Indians and white people, which in quantity consisted of about forty gallons that was thrown into the street." [75] The Shawnee further agreed to appoint four men to dispose of any rum or liquor brought into any Shawnee towns in the future, either by Indians or white men four a period of four years. The letter sent to Gordon was attached with a pledge signed by ninety-eight Shawnee men, as well as Chartier, and fellow trader George Miranda, that "no rum or strong liquor should be brought into their Towns for the term of four years." [76] Gordon evidently had no answer to this new development of the Ohio Shawnees directly banning rum. The new Governor, George Thomas would admit the cause of the terrible situation in the Ohio Country over the rum trade was due to lack of control in the past. Said Thomas to the Council in Philadelphia on July 31st 1744, "I cannot but be apprehensive that the Indian Trade as it is now carried on will involve us in some fatal Quarrel with the Indians. Our Traders in Defiance of the Law carry Spirituous Liquors amongst them, and take the Advantage of their inordinate Appetite for it to cheat them of their Skins and their Wampum, which is their Money, and often to debauch their Wives into the Bargain. Is it to be wondered at then, if when they Recover from the Drunken fit that they should take severe Revenges? I shall do all that is within my Power to prevent these Abuses by ordering a Strict Observance of the Law relating to Licenses, and the rigidest Prosecutions against such as shall be discovered to Sell Rum to the Indians. But I am Sensible these will avail but little; the ill practices of these people is carried on in the Woods, and at such a Distance from the Seat of Government that it will be very difficult to get Evidences to Convict them." [77]

The only question left was whether the rum traders would continue to ply their wares on the Ohio River in lieu of what amounted to a dire warning to them made by the Shawnee? By the time Thomas made his admission of failed policy to the Pennsylvania Council, it was too late. All out revolt against the rum traders by the Indians in the Ohio Country had begun. Peter Chartier sent a warning, for the last time, to the Pennsylvania Council with two traders, to no avail. The Governor rebuked Chartier, saying that his deposition was, "Some groundless insinuations of one Peter Chartier, an Indian trader." [78] The Governor's rebuff was the last straw for Chartier. By 1744, the Shawnee would begin to move far down the Ohio River to the Scioto, and Chartier's Town would be abandoned. In 1745, after waylaying a considerable number of rum traders and stripping them of their furs in retaliation for their robbery of the Indians, Peter Chartier would join his people, and turn his back on the English once and for all, whom he believed had a vested interest in destroying the Shawnee with rum, just as the French were renewing their presence in the Ohio Country. [79]

Would the Indians resort to violence to stop the rum traders? In response, would these unscrupulous white men who had operated with impunity for so long, kill Indians if they had to? Time would tell. But an ominous report came to the Governor of Pennsylvania in early June of 1743. A rumor was circulating among the traders to the Indians in the Ohio Country. Their Indian friends were telling them that they should "make the best of their Way out of Indian Country, to avoid their being murdered by the Indians, who were come to a Resolution to cut off all the white people." A terrible event had occurred the previous fall, on the "Alligheny" [Ohio River] that changed everything. An employee of an unnamed trader in the Ohio Country, presumably a rum trader, made a deposition before a justice that explained what had happened, as far as the traders were concerned. James Hendricks stated that, "He had seen the Indians there in pursuit of some of the Traders, And that he had heard the discharge of two or more Guns, from whence he verily believed that the pursued Traders were murdered." [80]

Part Two:
The Story

Place of the Skull

Chapter 6: The Indians

The young Lenape girl could not go back to sleep. The same dream had awakened her. It was a very simple dream she could remember. In the dream, she was lying on her back, looking up at the limbs of a big tree. The girl lay quietly awake, between the woolen trader blanket and the bearskin. She could hear the winter wind whistle through the trees outside the lodge like a mournful cry. Somewhere, a wolf howled in the distance. Turning her body once more to the glimmer of light coming from the fire pit coals, she felt her mother stir next to her, and nudged her awake. Whispering to her mother, she told her that she could not sleep, again. Concerned, her mother sat up on the bed bench and began stroking her daughter's head and running her fingers through her long black hair to comfort her and distract her mind from whatever was troubling her. As she had done in the past, Shakes-Her-Fist's mother began to tell her daughter the story of how their family had come with their clan people from across the mountains when Shakes-Her-Fist was still asleep in her belly. It was a story her daughter had heard before; but one that never grew old. As she began to retell it, she could see Shakes-Her-Fist listening intently in the dark.

She began the story saying that she had lived with her family and her husband, Shakes-Her-Fist's father, in the valley of the great Susquehanna River, in a small Lenape village of two dozen families very near to the large Lenape village of Schahamokink, meaning, "The place of the eels in the river." "The white traders called the village Shamokin, however, many Lenape believed the name to mean "The place of the chiefs, or rulers." This was because not only did the headman of the Delaware reside there, but the chief of the Iroquois as well. The leader of their people was a wise man who was named Allummapees, but many called him Sassounan. He ruled over their people there, the Unalachtigo, known as Turkey Clan Lenape, for as long as she could remember which was when she was a little girl herself. But all was not well with the Lenape, and many councils were held with the Elders to talk about the troubles that were not going away. There were more and more Lenape crowding into the village from the far-away Delaware River Valley seeking a new home away from the whites who kept taking more and more Lenape land for their own. The Iroquois themselves laid claim to all the land as far as anyone could see since the end of the wars with the Susquehannocks, but they were selling the land that the Lenape were standing on to the whites, calling the Lenape people women who wear skirts."

"Too, the village had seen much trouble with the English traders. While they brought the Lenape all the things that we wanted and needed to hunt, cook, sew, and dress ourselves, they brought the rum liquor too, which drove our men mad with a demon inside the kegs. This made the women run and hide in the woods until the drinking was over, and the traders gone, only to find that everyone's' possessions had been traded away during the night for more of the white man's evil water. This caused the Elders of the village great worry, and so they smoked many pipes of tobacco, and talked about what they should do. Then the day came when we heard that the Elders had come to a decision with much sadness. Most of the Unalachtigo and Unami, the Turkey and Turtle Clan Lenape wanted to leave and head west across the mountains, to the place where their people fished in the autumn on the river known as the Allegheny. The Munsee or Wolf Clan Lenape decided they would stay. And so it began some eight years ago.

Our close families packed our essential possessions and began walking the trail north along the west branch of the Susquehanna, following the east side of the river to the Lenape village of Sheshekwan, or Place of the Gourd Rattle."

"There, after a brief rest, we followed the well-worn ancient trail across mountains and fording rivers until reaching the old Lenape village of Cinguaklakamoose, or Place of the Large Laughing Moose. The trip was very hard for me. I was heavy with you and the long walk made my back and legs hurt. However, when we reached the Cowanshannock Creek, the trail was easier and led us down to the great Oh-Yee-O, at the Lenape village of Kittan, which means, "At the Great Stream." It was there that we rested and put our belongings down, and were fed by people who had already come from Shamokin. And after a day of resting, you began to stir, and I knew that it was time for me and your father to greet you, and so you came out. We laughed at how perfect and small you appeared to be, but we could not help but notice that one hand was clasped into a fist, which you shook at us, as if you were angry that we had not let you sleep some more." Looking down at Shakes-Her-Fist, her mother could see that her eyes were closed and sleep had once more found her.

Shakes-Her-Fist grew rapidly as the years passed, and she took her place alongside her mother and the other women at the Lenape village learning the essentials of the work that women did. First, there were fields to be worked in the spring to prepare for the crops. Tilling the soil and planting the maize, potatoes, beans, pumpkins, cucumbers, squashes and melons required the efforts of all the women, including the young teen girls. It was backbreaking work, and once the seed was put into the ground, it needed watered when dry and weeded when overgrown. In addition, a woman had to jerk the animal meat when the men brought back to the village what they had hunted and trapped. Meat would be cut into strips and either dried on racks in the sun or smoked over a slow fire. Fur-bearing hides needed hand scraped with a knife to remove the remaining flesh and connective tissue attached to the skin, and then brained tanned, stretched and cured. Hides and furs were what were used to trade with the white traders for their goods and cloth items when they came to the village. Food needed stored away for the winter for the time when it would be scarce.

Also, food needed prepared daily for all the extended family to eat. Firewood had to be hauled from the deep woods to the village and fires tended when the cooking pots were filled. Babies and young children needed cared for by the women until they were old enough to walk, and even then a woman always had to keep an eye on the toddlers that they did not fall in the river, wander off, or be bitten by snakes or a variety of other animals lurking nearby, including the village dogs. The wigwams, lodges, and cabins that the men had built were in constant need of repair to caulk holes and leaks to the bark walls and roofs. Occasionally when a new lodge needed built; it was the women who helped the men strip the bark off the elm to be made into slabs for the outside covering. Cattails needed gathered from the riverbanks and swampy areas to be woven into mats to sleep on. When there was time, a woman would sew clothes and moccasins for everyone and make herself presentable for her husband, if she were married. It was a hard life for a Lenape woman. Makes-A-Fist stepped into her mother's shoes and became known among the local Lenape as a hard-worker, equal to her mother.

By the time Shakes-Her-Fist was fourteen years, her mother could see that her daughter was becoming a woman, and attracting attention of the young men who were beginning to bring her little gifts of food and ribbon to seek her attention. Occupied as she was with another pregnancy and her daily chores, Shakes-Her-Fist's mother still had not failed to notice this. Shakes-Her-Fist as of late had taken to rubbing her long full black hair with bear grease to make it shine, which she had not done at any time in the past. Too, her mother noticed that Shakes-Her-Fist was now tying her shirt with a small strip of elm bark. It accentuated her slender waist and full hips which caught the eye of many young men who passed her in the fields. And there was another peculiar thing that Shakes-Her-Fist's mother noticed. Her daughter did not seem to be working as hard as she had previously, as time was now taken with her eyes, though modestly averted, looking at the young men cavorting her way. When she was scolded for this by her mother, Shakes-Her-Fist blushed with embarrassment. Her mother now knew that it would not be long before she would need to seek out a husband for Shakes-Her-Fist. He would need to be, above all else, a good hunter and warrior, more than simply a handsome man. Mother would not allow one of these frivolous young men of no standing to take her daughter. A husband must have a gun and ammunition, a canoe, spear, hatchet, a knife, looking glass and vermillion paint, a pipe and tobacco, a worthy bag and a knot-bowl to toss dice in. Shakes-her-Fist's mother wanted the very best for her daughter as she knew she had raised her the right way, the traditional way of the Lenape. Already everyone could see that she was a capable young woman who could sew, lace snow shoes, string wampum belts, work in the fields, boil the kettle and make moccasins.

The opportunity for Shakes-Her-Fist came three years later after the family had moved farther down the O-Yee-O River to a new village. Kittanning had become too crowded as more and more Lenape were arriving from the east to escape deplorable conditions there, as white people swarmed into former Lenape lands and took it for themselves, abusing all Indians. There was less food, firewood, fields to till, and breathing space at Kittanning any longer and many families were moving on to new places to live. Too, the rum traders had found their way to the Lenape's new home at Kittanning, and they plied there evil water just as they had done at Shamokin, and no one seemed able to stop them. She was now beginning to see young men who should be away hunting lying about the town in a drunken state, cursing and fighting with each other, and even drawing blood. The village did not bode well for her. She worried about many things, including Shakes-Her-Fist in the midst of the rum traders and drunken Lenape who were known to abuse women in the village, and even violate them. Quietly she went to her husband with her worries, and soon it was decided that they move down river, with several other close families, to a better place to live. After a brief stop at Shannopin's Town above the Forks of O-Yee-O and then the place called by the English trader's Logstown, a Shawnee and Lenape village, they continued to a Lenape village of several dozen lodges and families. It was there that Shakes-Her-Fist met Little Skunk.

The village lay on the north side of the O-Yee-O a half a day's journey from Shannopin's Town. The Lenape called it Amahknanne, which meant Beaver Stream, and it was here that Shakes-Her-Fist and her family decided to stop. Shakes-Her-Fist's father had a brother already living there, so it was a good place for them to re-unite since leaving Shamokin years ago.

Staying in the village were a few welcome Shawnee originally from across the mountains, as well as a family of Seneca who were great hunters, and therefore welcomed to reside there. The Lenape living there were all Unalachtigo Turkey clan of the same blood. It made for a good fit. The Seneca family was from up north, part of the *Honnat haiion'n*, or Wolf clan. The mother was a Delaware raised as a child by the Seneca who adopted her. The father was originally from the Seneca village named Guneunga which means "A Long Strip" referring to the long strip of bottom land that the Seneca farmed, where the upper O-Yee-O River was joined by Conewango. They were part of the continuing migration of the Seneca, Cayuga and Oneida who were moving into the valley of the Great River to make a life for themselves. Together, the mother and father had three children, and one of them, the eldest, was Little Skunk, who took early notice of Shakes-Her-Fist, soon after their arrival.

Little Skunk was several years older than Shakes-Her-Fist. When she first laid eyes on him she thought him not particularly handsome, and his quiet demeanor she took for shyness, perhaps as a result of his shorter height among the other boys. But she soon found that to be wrong. Little Skunk had indeed been given his name because of his size when he was born. He was small as a child, and so his mother named him Little Skunk after the animal that is not big, but is to be avoided because of its great strength that the Great Spirit had given it to offset its slightness in the woods. As Little Skunk grew, although shorter than the other boys his age, he was very sturdily built, and quick and light on his feet, and so able to outrun his playmates. But Little Skunk did not run away from those who teased him. Quiet and serious by nature, he stood his ground and fought all comers who wished to bully him. Once

Little Skunk planted his sturdy legs, no one was able to knock him off his feet. By the time he was twelve years, the bullying stopped. Little Skunk might be a head shorter than the rest of the young men, but he was a force to be reckoned with that no one dared to challenge without getting the worse of it for scratches, bruises, black eyes, and bloody noses. Little Skunk had become broad across the chest, with a narrow waist and muscles that rippled.

Though still considered a very young man, Shakes-Her-Fist learned that Little Skunk had already proven himself as an accomplished warrior in battle where most of the young men his age had not. The previous summer Little Skunk had asked to join his father and the other men in the war party. His father had refused, but undaunted, with a firm eye and voice, Little Skunk had petitioned the village Elders by displaying to them his ability to shoot bow and arrow, and swing a war club. At first wary to give their approval, Little Skunk convincing brought a fat deer that he just killed to the door of the council lodge as a gift to the Elders, and proof of his prowess. The Elders relented, and Little Skunk was allowed to take his place with the Iroquois war party headed south down the Catawba War Path into the lands the English called Virginia, Tennessee and the Carolinas, to wage war against their ancestral enemies, the Catawba and the Cherokee.

The war party of twelve men had taken their time to prepare. Several Cherokee scalps won in battle the previous year were hung from the red post in the village center. The warriors in their party painted themselves with vermillion and black, and plucked the hair on their heads except for a scalp lock on the crown of their heads, which they tied and decorated. This Little Skunk did as well. A war dance was performed by the warriors around the post set in the ground, and as each man circled the post singing his war song, he struck the post with his club or hatchet. With the singing and dancing over, the warriors crowded around the leader of the war party, who, in this case, was Little Skunk's uncle, his father's older brother, who, by calling for the war party, and having killed many of the enemy in the past, was made the captain by the Elders. It was at this time that Uncle told everyone assembled how and when they were to march, and where he hoped to strike the Cherokee, if good fortune prevailed.

They set out in the morning, in single file, with Little Skunk near the end. As the warriors left the village, they fired their guns off one by one, from front to rear, giving the war cry, and then singing the travelling song, *Hoo caugh-tainte heegana.* Many days of brisk walking the paths passed in silence as their war party headed south into the mountains and finally into Cherokee lands. Each man brought his own weapons and a small pack with jerked meat and crushed corn in it, prepared by the women for the trip. As Little Skunk had no gun of his own, and none that his father or uncle could lend him, he brought his bow and quiver of arrows tipped with the heads he had made of scrap iron. In his belt he carried the wooden war club he had made himself from the knot of ash wood he carved and painted. Then once they neared enemy land, all talking ceased, and a scout was sent ahead to carefully search for any enemy ambushes. One warrior was posted far to the rear to ensure that they had not been discovered and were being followed. Days passed as the war party stealthily approached a Cherokee village from a vantage point off any trails where they could observe the motions of the enemy without being observed themselves till the captain gave the signal that an opportunity had arisen to strike some unsuspecting enemy hunters leaving the village.

When the Cherokee hunting party came opposite the concealed Iroquois warriors, Uncle gave the war whoop and the warriors who were spread out in a line parallel to the path let loose a volley of musket fire and then leaped as one upon the dazed and wounded Cherokee. Little Skunk let loose two arrows on an unsuspecting man in his late thirties, one of which found its mark in the man's ribs. Instantly, Little Skunk was upon him, swinging his war club against the man's head, and crushing his skull. Then the unexpected happened. Out of the corner of his eye, Little Skunk could see an enemy warrior turn towards him, raising the muzzle of his gun to shoot. He was a Cherokee close to Little Skunk's own age, and as he prepared to fire, he trembled for an instant, and hesitated, indicating to Little Skunk that although he possessed a finer weapon, he had had little practice with it in hunting or battle. Little Skunk deftly ducked as the gun went off wildly, and then parried the muzzle with his own war club, as the enemy grabbed the weapon with both hands and attempted to swing it. He never got that far. Little Skunk closed the short gap and the next blow from his club hit the young man squarely on the brow of his head, crushing the bone. Quickly, the war party killed the enemy wounded and took their scalps, of which two hung from Little Skunk's belt, dripping blood. In an instant, their war party melted into the forest, and put miles between themselves and the ambush site.

There had been more battles with the Cherokee, and warriors of their own had been wounded, but Little Skunk, his father, and his uncle were not one of them. Many of the enemy had been slain, and Little Skunk by his own hand had killed two. He took their scalps which he cleaned, strung on hoops, and painted to bring back with him as testament to his deed, and his courage as a warrior. In addition, several prisoners were captured and brought back to the village for the Elders to decide in they should be adopted, as was the custom. Little Skunk had become a man as a result. His bravery in battle was recognized by all, though he himself was not one to brag about it as some young warriors were taken to do, as they lazed around, smoking tobacco and playing with dice. Little Skunk was not one to sit still. He had accomplished much since returning from war, and was already a man with possessions resulting from his ability to hunt in the woods and bring back much meat and plenty of furs and hides for trade. Little Skunk had purchased his own gun and ammunition from the traders, and it was now rumored among the women that he was looking for a wife.

Thus it came as no surprise to Shakes-Her-Fist's mother when Little Skunk came to their lodge one day as a suitor, seeking Shakes-Her-Fist consent to marriage. The two had spoken to each other on only a few occasions, and then only briefly, however, it was apparent that they had eyes for each other and no one else. With all the formality he could muster, Little Skunk dropped the cake of Indian bread into the lap of Shakes-Her-Fist, signifying that he was proposing marriage to her, as he found her a suitable mate. Shakes-Her-Fist picked up the bread, handling it fondly, and looked up into the eyes of Little Skunk, approvingly, with a smile. If she had tossed the cake of Indian bread aside, it would have meant that she disliked Little Skunk, and he should not return to her lodge again. But that did not happen. Her acceptance of Little Skunk meant that he could take her as a wife. The next morning, Little Skunk brought presents of a wool blanket, some strings of wampum, a spool of ribbon and two legs of venison to the lodge to

97

give to the parents of Shakes-Her-Fist, which were accepted. Then, Little Skunk's mother, father, sisters, uncle, and younger brother came to the lodge with food to celebrate the marriage with a feast. Soon after, Little Skunk busied himself with building a lodge of his own for himself and his new wife. The following spring of the year which the English traders called 1743, Little Skunk decided to move with his family and Shakes-Her-Fist further downriver, where Little Skunk had heard that the game was more plentiful up any of the many creeks and stream bottoms feeding into the O-Yee-O. If the hunting was much better, Little Skunk determined that the fur skins that could be taken would mean much in the trade goods he would need to support his family, which now included a son he hoped, who would be born before the first snows fell.

Chapter 7: A Rum Trader Named Dunning

James Dunning paced back and forth between the horses and his waiting men, to the edge of the barn within eyeshot of John Harris's trading cabin about four hundred feet away. Not a patient man when it came to taking risks, Dunning wondered if something had gone wrong, since nothing, it seemed, about this particular jaunt, had been going right up to this point. Harris knew that they had to get loaded and on their way at dark, while the moon was highest, so as to make it past Le Tort's several miles up ahead, to the spring at Mount Rock. There, they could rest for the night at his brother, Robert's cabin, and get a good start on the mountains in the early morning, headed for Trader's Gap. Robert had an Indian squaw who would have food ready for them. It was just a matter of getting the horses loaded and the four men with him in the saddle. Hendricks was his best man out of the lot of them. He had seen to the problems with the horses and their saddle packs. But as to the rest of them, Dunning knew they were slim pickings when he and Hendricks fished them out of the tavern in Paxtang across the river, and hired them. They tried their best to sober them up, and got them across the Susquehanna with only Fitzpatrick falling out of his saddle, drunk, into the river. Fitzpatrick, a Scotch-Irish from Ulster County, was not a man Dunning cared to deal with when he was sober, much less drunk. A growling, irascible sort, who cared little for taking orders from anyone, he constantly spit a stream of tobacco juice through the gaps in his rotten teeth, when spoken to. He was a man of little words, which enamored him little to anyone, and right now he was still drunk. Dunning had sized Fitzpatrick up. He might be a tough piece of gristle to handle, but Fitzpatrick was no coward. A good fighter in a tight spot with the Injuns, if that should happen. John McAfee, on the other hand, struck Dunning as a weak, shifting sort; but good with horses, everyone said. Dunning had yet to see it.

Quinn; now he was another matter. A total, vile, inveterate alcoholic, Dunning supposed. Good with a knife, Dunning had heard. Good enough to cut a man open from stem to stern like a military surgeon some rumored. Not a man to be fooled with if he were in a foul mood, which he usually was when it came to rum. And right now Quinn looked like he needed a drink in a bad way. Dunning told himself he'd have to keep his eye on Quinn. Anything might happen if he ever got sober enough between binges and took a dislike to any one of them. They were a motley lot for him and Hendricks to handle, Dunning told himself, but they'd have to do, at this point. He couldn't wait any longer to make it for the Ohio Country, and the Miami Indians down the Ohio. All the word coming this way from Indian country said that Chartier had the Shawnee all stirred up and looking for rum traders, in particular, to lift their liquor, furs skins, and scalps. Dunning knew exactly what that meant. His scalp. He and that Frenchman had never seen eye-to-eye on anything, and Dunning chalked it up to Chartier's Injun blood: he was more Injun than them Shawnee themselves. They looked up to him, and did most all of what he told them to do. Chartier had put the word out to the other traders that he was going to find Dunning and get him. Chartier was hell-bent on saving the Shawnee from the likes of Dunning and his rum. Chartier knew something that Dunning knew. Chartier knew that Dunning would be back. To Chartier, it was just a matter of where and when he and the Shawnee would catch up with him. That wouldn't happen if

Dunning had a say in it. Yes, he was coming back, but a fool he was not.

The senior John Harris finally showed up with his young son carrying the lanterns. The delay was unfortunate, but necessary, Harris explained, as he opened the rear door of the barn facing the hillside, away from prying eyes. A justice and his deputy had ridden in from across the Susquehanna just at dusk, asking a lot of questions. Harris had no choice but to oblige them. They wanted to know if he had seen or heard of a man going by the name Thomas Smyth. The justice didn't believe Smyth to be his real name, but he knew what he looked like and gave a detailed description. Smyth was wanted by colony authorities. He had cut an Indian woman up real bad down at Conestoga in a drunken brawl about two weeks ago. When she died, Smyth disappeared and word had it he was headed west. A warrant was out for his arrest. Harris shook his head in disgust, and told the justice that had not seen him pass his way. Then there was the matter of a man named Timothy Fitzpatrick, Harris recounted. Seems that the justice wanted to question him about some missing property that he was alleged to have misappropriated in Paxtang from an Indian trader named Edward Kenny. Both Dunning and Harris knew Kenny, and laughed. "So a thief stealing from another thief? Ole Kenny must be slipping these days to let someone slip a keg of rum from under his nose," chuckled Dunning. Shooting a glance Fitzpatrick's way, who was helping the others load the eight gallon kegs of rum on the horses' saddle racks, Dunning asked what this Fitzpatrick looked like, but Harris said that no one knew. No, Dunning replied to Harris, he had not seen or heard of such a man, thinking to himself that it didn't pay to let Harris in on too much. Dealing with him on rum was one thing: trusting him was another, and Dunning was not about to take a chance of saying something when he didn't have to. If Harris's double-dealing ever got him in trouble, he might do a lot of talking.

One other thing Harris said the justice had on his mind. He had a message for Harris to give Dunning if he should run into him. It seemed the new governor of the province, George Thomas, wanted to talk to him. Thomas was not like Gordon, the previous governor. Things were changing both inside and out of the province, especially with the Indians, and Thomas was of the mind that the traders were making as many enemies as friends with the Indians, especially over the mountains. And now there were rumors reaching Philadelphia that the French were showing some interest in the Ohio Country as of late, thanks to Peter Chartier. Thomas wanted to get a handle on it. He was calling in all the experienced traders to talk to him, and he wanted to talk to Dunning. Dunning the Irishman who knew all the trails; Dunning the experienced trader with the Indians; Dunning the trader without a license and Dunning the man with the allegation of good trader gone the way of rum running hanging over his head. The justice said it was best Dunning come in while he still could show his face. Harris should tell him that if he seen him.

Dunning looked into Harris's concerned face but had no response for him. He would think about it after this trip to the Ohio was over, but not now. Not since Harris wanted payment for the sixty gallons of rum in hard currency. "Sorry, but no credit anymore for rum traders, not even you. The risks are too great now, even for me. Going to get out this business," said Harris. Dunning shrugged. He knew Harris well enough to know the greed that drove the man was not likely to stop anytime soon. Dunning handed the shillings over to

Harris without comment. He also knew all too well what Harris meant when he added, "Too risky with the Injuns all up in arms." The risk was coming back empty-handed with no furs and no rum. And better yet, no scalp, Dunning thought. With the horses loaded and the kegs covered, Dunning nodded goodbye to Harris, and he and his men headed off along the well-worn trail to the west in the moonlight.

Dunning and his men passed Le Tort's cabin during the night and got to Robert's without much delay and were now on their way along the path through Trader's Gap. An incident had happened at Robert's that troubled Dunning. Quinn had drank a good deal of rum at the table and then taken an interest in the Indian squaw who was Robert's household help while his wife was sick. Quinn wouldn't leave her alone, until Robert intervened. Robert had words with Quinn who reached for his knife, but didn't pull it. Dunning took him outside and gave him a tongue-lashing, and Quinn mumbled an apology and it was over. But it worried Dunning; a worry he didn't need to have added to his list at this time. First and foremost, Dunning needed to get his men and horses into the mountains and through the Trader's Gap. From that point on, there were many paths they could follow up to Tuscarora Hill which was more than thirty miles. Dunning knew they could not make it in one day on the rough path that wound up and down for some distance. It would be laborious work; and take several days at best. They would have to ford several streams, including the Conodoguinet River after going through Trader's Gap. Dunning stopped the horses and had the men tighten the cinches on all the horse saddle packs since the weight that each pack horse carried was two eight-gallon rum kegs each weighing about seventy pounds. From there on, the path ascending Kittatinny Mountain was exceptionally tough on the horses due to the slippery shale rock. Dunning had the men dismount and walk the string of pack horses up the grade to keep them from losing their footing. With luck and good weather, Dunning hoped he and his men would get to the Juniata River crossing that John Wray had told him about. It was there an old Indian path headed west to the Ohio and Shannopin's Town, avoiding Kittanning and the Shawnee across the Allegheny at Chartier's village. Hopefully, they could avoid the Shawnee altogether.

The second worry on Dunning's mind as the days wore on was the lack of forage for the horses. He had made sure that some hay and oats was packed away with their own provisions, but there was nothing for the horses to eat in the woods when they camped for the night. It was too early in the year for much of anything to grow, much less under the tall trees that let in little sunlight once they leaved. Dunning was reluctant to let the horses try to graze freely for whatever little they could find, knowing from the howling he heard from time to time that wolves were not too far off. Too, if even one horse were lost, the others would not be able to carry its two kegs of rum. The cargo was just too valuable to take that chance. By the next day, they made it up the short, steep path to Shadow of Death, and then three more miles down to the creek and then back up through the Narrows of Blacklog Mountain, where they stopped at a sleeping place off the path. It had been a miserable day. A hard, long rain had soaked them all to the skin before stopping, making it difficult to find wood for a fire to dry out. The horses were hungry and there was nothing for them to eat. They had not seen anyone except an old Indian who gave them a wide berth outside the range of their muskets as they passed. That did not bode well, Dunning thought. Obviously the Indian knew who they were and what they were carrying under the linen tarpaulins. The men grumbled when Dunning ordered that the horses be unloaded for the night. He didn't want the horses becoming lame from the more than 150 pounds on their backs, but it was a chore no one relished. It took two men to untie and lift the kegs down easily, and they grunted and swore with each one. The next morning they left the main path that turned to the north up the Aughwick Creek Valley towards the northwest, and Kittanning. Instead, Dunning turned to the southwest, following a smaller, less-used path that wound its way through towering forests to the crest of the high, narrow, Side Long mountain and then down to the west branch of the Juniata River far below.

It was at the Juniata ford that trouble arose. Dunning discovered that there were Indians camped there at the shallows when he and his men made their way down to the river. It was a hunting camp, Dunning guessed, of mixed Delaware and a few Shawnee and that's what worried him. Not that he figured they would give him any trouble there, but it was obvious that the Shawnee had seen him, and they who he was. The Indians invited the traders to stay for the night, saying that they had food to share, and guess that the traders had rum. Dunning whispered to his men that they were going to push on without stopping after the barest of greetings had been made, and Dunning lied and told the Indians that he hoped to make the Warrior's Path ahead in due time, and get his load of supplies up to Kittanning before the Indians left for hunting. The Indians said they understood, but Dunning knew he had fooled no one. They knew correctly that he was carrying rum and they asked again if he had any to spare. Shaking his head, Dunning tossed them a twist of tobacco and tipped his hat while keeping his men and horses moving west all the time, till he found a suitable place to camp and rest the horses for the night.

After following a narrow ridge for several miles the next morning, between the loops made by the Juniata River, the men and horses descended the path and made a second crossing at a ford. The place was deserted, save strong evidence everywhere of Indian hunting camps made over the years. Nearby, Dunning found the spot where John Wray had made a lean-to shelter. Wray told Dunning back in Paxtang that he hoped to build a trading cabin there soon. Close at hand was the intersection of paths Wray told him about. The Warrior's Path ran north to Kittanning and south through the mountains to Maryland, and had been used by the Iroquois for generations to wage war against the Catawba and Cherokee. Dunning could see why Wray liked the spot. There was plenty of good water, and some open ground for horses to forage, meaning, Wray could keep his own horses here without worrying about them starving. In the morning when the men loaded the rum kegs once again, Dunning noticed that the cargo on the last horse was listed to one side. As he went to adjust it, Dunning discovered that the particular keg on the upper side of the horse was lighter than usual, telling him immediately that, with nothing leaking from the keg, someone had been tapping it unbeknownst to anyone. Dunning called the men around him and it didn't take long to ferret the culprit out. Quinn was the only man with the smell of liquor on his breath.

Dunning was furious; his temper boiled white hot. On any other occasion he might beat Quinn to a bloody pulp, or worse. Yet here, he was having a difficult time restraining himself, knowing instinctively that he needed Quinn's services as yet. Quinn never uttered a word as Dunning railed, but as he had done in the past when someone confronted him beyond the little that he could bear, Quinn reached for his knife which was a mistake. He never got it out of its sheath.

Dunning caught Quinn first with a hard knuckle blow to the chin that sent him reeling backwards. A couple of kicks by Dunning to Quinn's mid-section convinced the man to quickly submit before Dunning went farther. Dunning dictated the terms to Quinn. If he needed rum that bad, Dunning would dole some out to him till they reached the Ohio and Shannopin's where they would stay for a couple of days, and Quinn could do what he wanted. Until then, his drink would be restricted by Dunning, and it would cost him part of the profits Dunning promised him. Without any cards to bargain with, Quinn nodded his head and rubbed his aching jaw. Dunning hoped it would be a reminder to the man, and anyone else, that he would tolerate no more trouble while they were on the trail.

From the Warrior's Path, the trail headed in a general westerly direction, as it approached the looming Allegheny Mountain that could be seen in the distance through the trees. Gradually, the path began the climb to the summit, after they passed the site of the old Shawnee cabins, now deserted, about eight miles from Wray's lean-to. Dunning believed that the place had been a stopping point for the Shawnee when the migrated west from their Old Town on the Potomac River in Maryland some years ago. It must have been a village at one time, Dunning reckoned, by the number of arrowheads and chips strewn about the ground at the nearby creek bank. The Shawnee weren't making arrowheads any longer, at least not out of stone, Dunning told the men. From the Shawnee cabins to the summit of the mountain ahead was a steep and narrow climb for the horses. It was made all the more difficult by the fact that the horses were weakened by the past ten days of strenuous work without much to eat. Hendricks pointed out that they looked particularly thin, at this point, which Dunning could see. Nearing the summit, a steady rain that had been falling turned to sleet, and then snow, soaking everyone to the skin. Upon reaching the summit, they were all miserably wet and cold, with no wood anywhere dry enough to kindle a fire. Dunning, however, suggested they keep moving and dry out once they crossed the mountain. From the summit, the path split and Dunning took the southern fork, knowing that the northern path would be too steep for the horses, which could easily tumble down the hillsides or break legs. Dunning chose the route that was wetter, and crossed a series of streams, but the grade of the path was gentler, though he was told, longer. After several miles, the two paths came together again on the summit of the last major mountain standing in their way to the Ohio. Dunning could finally breathe a sigh of relief that he and his men were mostly over the mountains without losing any of their precious load. The worst of the trip was over, Dunning hoped, as long as the Shawnee they passed had not sent someone to Kittanning on the northern path to alert Chartier.

The next few days were routine. The path followed more gently rolling hills that were soft, with no stone to cut the horse's hoofs as the mountains had. Dunning took the path that led through the valley made by Loyal Hanna Creek, a tributary that Dunning knew flowed into the Kee-ak-kshee-man-nit-toos River, which meant "Place of the Cut Spirit" to the Delaware. Its outlet would bring a traveller to the Ohio, opposite Chartier's Town. There was a Delaware village at Loyal Hanna, but not many people were home when Dunning and his men arrived. It was a good place to spend the night. Dunning knew some of the villagers from earlier trades on the Ohio, which was only fifty miles away. Dunning and his men had a chance to rest the next day, and they took advantage of it. He had Hendricks see to the horses, and get feed from the Indians in exchange for a few trade goods Dunning had had the foresight to bring along, and a small keg of rum of his own. In the evening, with the horses and goods secured, Dunning had a chance to relax around a fire with some of the Delaware men. They smoked a few pipes of tobacco, drank a draught of rum and exchanged the news that each man had to tell, in their own turn. Events, Dunning heard, were tumultuous on the Ohio. There had been a number of robberies up and down the river, and more than a few drunken sprees that were spectacles. A Frenchman had come down the river recently, speaking to the Indians about new traders soon to come from Montreal. Dunning took it all in, and shared what news he had, not forgetting to ask about Chartier and a man named Smyth too. In the meantime, Hendricks had gone to his bedding, Fitzpatrick amused himself with a Delaware squaw, and Quinn drank himself into a stupor with the rum he had left. McAfee, ever the loner, kept to himself, keeping watch over the horses and rum.

As they were saddling up the horses the next morning, a Delaware Indian whom Dunning was familiar with strolled over to him as he packed his bedroll. Speaking in the Lenape tongue, the Indian told him that he was sure he had seen the man with the horses named McAfee before, and that he wanted Dunning to know. McAfee had been working for Chartier at Kittanning, unloading skins from a canoe that Chartier was sending with him and a few others to the East. Without further words, the Indian nodded at Dunning and left. Dunning was thankful for the information. He paused from his work to toss what he had been told around in his head, finally deciding to himself that he was better off not confronting McAfee as a spy for Chartier. The man would deny it anyway and never let Dunning know what he was up to. It was better for Dunning to keep his eye on McAfee and wait to see if he let his guard down, or made a mistake and revealed his real intentions to someone else in the crew who would undoubtedly let Dunning know, rather than risk their share of the profits. Once the horses were ready, they headed west on the beaten path. The final leg of the trip would take two days to cover before reaching the village above the Forks of the Ohio that the Delaware called Diondega, or Shannopin's Town.

The previous two days' journey had been gratefully uneventful for Dunning; although the suspense kept building the closer they got to the Ohio. Dunning was unsure what he was about to find at Shannopin's. He hoped the old Delaware chief would be there and in good spirits. Dunning knew Shannopin well. They had met on several occasions, smoked pipe, drank liquor and played dice, and laughed at each other's stories. Shannopin had been a great orator with a gift for words, and a story-teller in his own right, in addition to being a good-natured and sincere Indian. But that was the old days before the liquor traders had debauched him. Shannopin was now but a shadow of his old self; rarely clear-headed, and most often found drunk. His once sizable collection of possessions, including lodges, guns, goods, horses, and wives had been shamefully squandered on rum, and Dunning knew if he seen the old man again, it would probably be his last. Dunning was shocked to find when they finally entered the village with its mish-mash of cabins, lodges, and huts sitting up on the bluff above the river, that the so-called Town had grown since he had seen it last, two years ago. There were more Indians from various tribes than he could recall, and more English traders with horse pens, beached canoes, storage cabins and greasy, grimy, bearded men than he could imagine. The pall of smoke and stench from dozens of cooking fires roasting a variety of meat was overwhelming. Most important of all, as Dunning scanned the village one more time before looking for Shannopin, the long, black-haired Chartier and his Shawnee were nowhere to be seen.

Dunning made sure Hendricks had the men secure the horses and cargo before he allowed them to look for food and entertainment. Shannopin was where Dunning supposed him to be, and then two men hugged as genuine friends, happy to see that the other was still living. After catching up on the news, Dunning knew the protocol if Shannopin was going to extend hospitality to Dunning and his men, and give his approval for Dunning to conduct the trade of horses for canoes that needed to be done. They got down to business in spite of the fact that the old Delaware was mildly drunk. Dunning helped Hendricks bring one of the kegs of rum over to Shannopin's cabin and placed it near the door as collateral for the haggling to begin. Dunning knew his horses were played out; near starvation. If Shannopin agreed to allow Dunning to exchange the horses for two large canoes to take his cargo downriver, which Dunning was sure he would, it was just a matter of the cost. Shannopin would see that the horses were fed, watered, and secured from thieves while Dunning was gone. In return, Shannopin wanted a share of the profits Dunning hoped to return with. If Dunning did not return with the canoes, or furs, he forfeited his eight pack-horses and five others to Shannopin, which were ten times the value of the canoes. If he did return, Shannopin wanted a percentage of the skins, to be determined when he inspected them.

Dunning shook on the deal, knowing it was fair. However, as an added thought, Shannopin wanted a keg of rum thrown in as a sign of their longstanding friendship, to seal the deal. Dunning protested. A keg of eight gallons of rum was too much; reminding

Shannopin that four gallons was part of the deal in the past. Shannopin slowly shook his head. Much had changed, he reminded Dunning. The deals of the past were in the past. Deals with rum traders were hard to come by these days for men like Dunning, with so many Indians wishing him ill, like Chartier. Shannopin was willing to take the risk one more time, but his cost of doing business for such risk as Dunning was asking, had gone up. Dunning thought it over. He had ten eight-gallon kegs that had been carried on five pack-horses evenly. Quinn had tapped into one of them on the trip over the mountains. Now he would give up a full keg to the Indian which would leave him with little over eight and a half. He had been counting on the initial cost of doing business with the chief at four gallons. This was a new wrinkle. To make the trade with the Miamis exceedingly profitable, Dunning would now have to squeeze them a little tighter, and he didn't like that idea, especially with Shannopin encouraging it. Dunning knew there would be no love lost on Shannopin's part if the dealing fell through with the Miamis because of him. Shannopin would win. He'd get Dunning's horses and the keg of rum for two leaky canoes. Finally done mulling it over, Dunning relented, shrugging his shoulders. It irked him that at the moment, he needed the wily old Delaware more the Indian needed him. Unless, of course, Shannopin needed him dead at Chartier's urging. These Indians might fight with each other but there blood was thicker than water when it came to their dislike of the white man, he thought.

While Dunning pondered the possibility that the old chief whom he liked, but didn't trust, might find it in his interest to see him dead, a raucous brawl involving the white traders at a nearby fire caught Dunning's attention. Just as Shannopin was opening his new keg of rum, Quinn came running up, yelling that Fitzpatrick was hurt real bad. Dunning ran over to find out what happened. It seemed that none other than Edward Kenny, the man whom Fitzpatrick was alleged to have robbed in Paxtang, appeared out of nowhere and confronted Fitzpatrick with a drawn knife. Fitzpatrick responded in kind, and the two men slashed at each other until Kenny had the meat on his left leg opened up to the bone by Fitzpatrick. The problem was that one of Kenny's associates then pushed Fitzpatrick backwards into the roaring fire, whereupon he was badly burned on his back, neck and shoulders before he was able to roll himself out. Fitzpatrick was writhing in agony; the normally tight-lipped Scotch-Irishman was shrieking from the pain. Dunning helped with the removal of Fitzpatrick's smoldering shirts, and summoned one of Shannopin's women to help clean the blistered, charred flesh and apply a salve and poultice. It was questionable in Dunning's mind whether Fitzpatrick would survive. Already he was in shock from the injury, and shaking uncontrollably. If the man did make it, he would need weeks to heal enough to the point he could travel. The smell of Fitzpatrick's roasted human flesh was disgusting; and brought a twinge of nausea to Dunning that made him want to wretch. He was reminded of the stories of men being slowly roasted alive by the Indians, as was their practice in time of war. Quickly Dunning put that thought out of his mind, and tried not to listen to the agonizing cries of Fitzpatrick, who was beyond his help at the moment.

"Where would he find another man to replace Fitzpatrick," Dunning asked himself, trying to keep his mind on the problem at hand. He had wanted to leave down the Ohio in the next day or two at best, and now he was short one man who could not be spared on any account. Dunning cursed at his bad luck, remembering that he had once thought before setting out on this jaunt that it could be ill-fated. It was precisely at that moment that Shannopin motioned for Dunning to come over to him. Shannopin, now thoroughly drunk but possessing some of his faculties, had been taking in the whole spectacle from the door of his cabin where we was seated with several warriors who were drinking rum, and roaring with laughter. It was as if Shannopin could read his mind, Dunning thought for a moment. Shannopin was pointing to one of his own employees who had his back turned to him. "I will loan you this white man here as part of our bargain. He is indebted to me. You need another hand and he is good with a paddle, like a Lenape," Shannopin slyly joked, as the white man turned to face Dunning. "Doon-ning, my friend, his name is Thoo-maas. Thoo-maas Smeth."

FATHER BONNECAMP'S MAP   1749

Father Bonnecamp's 1749 map of the Celeron
Expedition down the Ohio River. Note his phonetic
spelling of the Iroquois word "place of the skull." Note
also his phonetic spelling "Ranonouara" which is the
Iroquois word for "place of the skull."

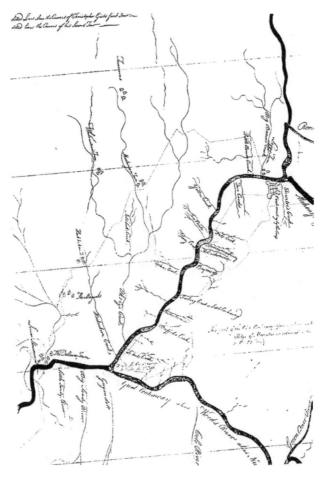

Mercer's 1752 map of Christopher Gist's 1750-1751
explorations of the Ohio River, and his notation "Scalp
Creek," an English translation of the Dalaware word for
"Weel-lunk."

The upper Ohio section of John Mitchell's 1755 map
noting "Scalp Creek."

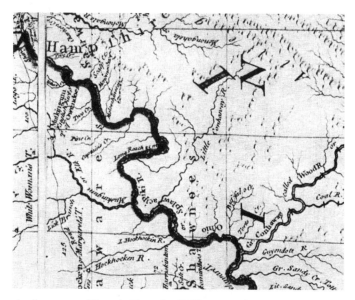

A close-up of Lewis Evan's 1755 map of the upper Ohio River noting "Weeling Creek" and "Weeling Island."

Chapter 8: The Fateful Event at That Place on the Ohio

Any doubts about Shannopin's loyalty were put to rest in Dunning's mind when the Indian offered Smyth's services. No doubt the Delaware was thinking about his profits yet to be realized if all went well for Dunning downriver. It was very much in his interests to supply the missing man to replace Fitzpatrick. Dunning had looked Smyth over. Thomas Smyth was a thin, wiry man with black greasy hair and piercing blue eyes; and like Fitzpatrick, Smyth, or whatever his name was, was a man of few words. Dunning asked Smyth directly if he was, in fact, the man that Pennsylvania authorities were looking for back in Paxtang over a squaw. Smyth, staring Dunning in the eye, did not flinch, nor explain or deny. All he said to Dunning was that he wouldn't be going back east anytime soon, and when he got back to Shannopin's, he still had something to work off with the Delaware head man. That was it. That was all Dunning needed to know. Smyth seemed solid enough to Dunning, and didn't waste any time proving his worth when it came to loading the two canoes. Some provisions for the trip that Dunning had purchased were added, and then Dunning said a last farewell to Shannopin, telling him that he hoped to be back in ten days if all went well. Shannopin, who was sober this morning, gave Dunning some last advice before he left. Dunning should pass by the Shawnee village at the mouth of the Scioto River on his way to the Twightees on the Big Miami River below the Scioto. No one knew exactly where Chartier was, at the moment. He could be there, Shannopin emphasized, waiting for Dunning. Dunning waved the chief off. He had already made up his mind to pass the Shawnee village at night, both coming and going, to avoid trouble. Wrestling those furs away from the Miamis and getting clean away without losing their scalps if the Indians should feel cheated was going to be enough trouble in itself without more.

Dunning and his men swung their wide loaded canoes into the Ohio River and began paddling for the main current of the river. What concerned Dunning the most was the unexpected. As much as he planned for it, something always managed to happen to surprise him when dealing with Indians. The Twightees, or Miamis as the English liked to call them, were touchy, Dunning recalled, from a previous trip downriver. There had been a squabble over a married Indian squaw that held everything up Dunning remembered. Perhaps, being the furthest away from the English traders at Logstown and Shannopin's, the Miamis just weren't well enough acquainted with the traders to know what to expect. Then there was the fact that there was not a lot of news reaching the traders as far as what these particular Indians were up to, which naturally put whites on edge. One never knew for sure how the Miamis might react, especially since it was rumored that the French from Detroit had been paying them visits, as of late. Dunning didn't know if that was Chartier's doing, or the result of the Miamis being that much closer in proximity to the French than the English. He would just have to wait and see, and let it all play out, while keeping his guard up and his eyes peeled for trouble, at all times. Dunning did know that the Miamis had been moving back into their home lands in the past years since the war with the Iroquois was over for good, and the Indians seemed genuinely friendly the last time Dunning had paid them a visit with Peter Tostee and the other traders. However, they brought guns, powder and lead that time; things the Miamis needed. This time would be different. If the

Indians broke the kegs open and got drunk on the spot, as Dunning expected might happen, all hell would break loose before they could get their newly purchased furs and deer skins loaded. It was a situation he wanted to avoid at all costs.

After a stop for the night at Logstown miles below the Forks, Dunning and his men got a good early start paddling down the Ohio the next morning. Dunning and Hendricks, the most experienced man of the bunch, were in one canoe with five of the kegs; the three others, Smyth, McAfee, and Quinn were in the other with the four other kegs, as well as the scant trade goods. Dunning made sure that the four muskets were equally divided between the two boats, and loaded just in case trouble might arrive. Paddling down river several hours below Logstown, they approached the island in the river that Dunning had passed before. He urged the men in the other canoe to take the left channel where the water was deepest, and avoid the right where they might all get hung up on the shallows where there was a fording place. Ahead he could see that there appeared to be Indians at the mouth of the creek flowing into the Ohio. On the north bank of that creek they had set up a hunting camp, Dunning figured, by what appeared to be drying racks for meat and hides. It was a good place to stop and hunt, Dunning thought to himself, perhaps on the trip back. As they passed the large island in the river, some elk and deer were spotted grazing close to the west bank of the Ohio, apparently out-of-view of the Indians on the other side of the Ohio. Without stopping, Dunning kept the men paddling down river.

Little Skunk, Shakes-Her-Fist and three other families had travelled downriver in canoes over two weeks ago, and set up temporary lean-to lodges on the site of the old hunting camp that lay next to the path the crossed the river and headed east. They beached their canoes on the creek bank beneath the large elm tree that overhung the creek, and began building drying racks for the hides and meat they hoped to bring in. The more than a dozen women and young girls busied themselves with securing the huts, as well as hauling in a sizable amount of seasoned wood from the surrounding forest that would be needed for their stay that might last several weeks. The young girls would tend to the babies, who were brought along, while the women and mothers planned to dry the meat and dress the hides as the hunters brought their catch in. On Little Skunk's urging, the men loaded their guns and followed the ancestral path that followed the north bank of the creek as it wound its way eastward. From the lay of the land which allowed only for a steep climb for any game animal wishing to escape them, Little Skunk believed that the hunt would be successful, and in fact, it was. The hunting had been especially good for the four men, and a half a dozen boys. Soon the women were hard at work preparing the elk, bear, deer hides. Shakes-Her-Fist worked alongside the other women scraping the animal hides, but it was evident to all that her heavy-with-child condition caused her to tire easily. As a result, she was sent to tend the cooking fire and preparing food for the men when they returned.

After camping at the mouth of the Muskingum River, and then the Hockhocking, Dunning had the men lay over several miles above the mouth of the Scioto River. They would wait for night to fall before passing, and then would tie the two canoes together end-to-end and allow them to drift downriver with minimal paddling. Dunning was not going to take any chances. If Chartier were there at the Shawnee village some called Lower Town, all the efforts made up to this point would be lost, knowing what Chartier and his Indians were capable of doing. However, Dunning's careful attention to detail worked. They quietly slipped by the Shawnee village situated on the banks of the Scioto during the night, and Dunning was sure they hadn't been spotted, as they waited for the quarter-moon to set and navigated the river by starlight. Another day and they would reach the mouth of the Little Miami River, and then less than half a day to the Big Miami River, and the village at its mouth. All was going well, so far, Dunning told the men. Now they would need to take great care to follow his instructions when they approached the mouth of the Miami. The canoe with McAfee, Quinn, and Smyth would stay to the opposite of the main channel of the Ohio and wait for Dunning's orders to cross the river. Meanwhile, he and Hendricks would paddle to the village at the mouth of the Big Miami, and Dunning would go ashore while Hendricks remained close by in the canoe.

Dunning told them that a multitude of English traders had already been coming to the string of Miami villages that stretched along the river, north into the Ohio Country. For two or more years, the traders had traveled the paths leading west from Logstown with their pack horses filled with a variety of goods, but little liquor. The Miamis were far from the English and closer to the French who had a fort on the Maumee River to the north, yet they had welcomed the English traders in the past because their goods were more plentiful, cheaper, and better quality than French trade goods. Dunning had met *Aquenackqua*, The Turtle, on his last and only trip up the Miami River, and Dunning would be fortunate to find the Miami chief again down in his village on the Ohio. At this time of the hunting season, the Turtle stayed in the lower village across from the Kan-Tuc-Kee lands. However, this visit was going to be all business, and everyone was going to follow the rules Dunning was about to set down. If he could strike the deal with the Miamis, then they would bring the canoes in, and unload, transferring the kegs for furs. No one but no one would enter the village and under no circumstances would they stay the night, no matter how exhausted. Striking any deal depended upon them putting some distance between them and the village once they were packed, even if it meant paddling upriver during the night. Their wages and their lives entirely depended upon it. It would only be a matter of time before the warriors got drunk, and most likely, once the women in the village came to understand what was happening, they would start gathering up everything they owned, including the children, and head for the woods to hideout. The Indians knew what liquor was. Some of it had got here by way of the traders on the trails. Now they were about to find out what a major drunk was, and a costly one at that. Dunning reiterated his warning intended for Smyth, McAfee, and Quinn. "I don't want you leavin the canoes for any reason, as I won't be waitin for ya, and the Indians will. Once they get sobered up, and come to their senses, they'll wanna roast ya alive to ease their throbbing heads."

Fortunately all had gone well. Dunning had found The Turtle and another Miami Chief, Cold Foot. A trade of rum for hides was agreed upon and Dunning was satisfied with the deal. Both canoes were loaded with bales of deer skins and elk hides and they managed to get underway in a timely manner, everyone breathing a sigh of relief when they reached the middle of the Ohio River and paddled out of sight of the Miamis. Though bulky, the canoes were somewhat lighter than the rum, which made paddling upriver manageable, though tiring. Dunning thought of the profits he would accrue back East once he paid off the men and his creditors for the supplies and meager Indian goods that he had brought along. Shannopin would want a share of the skins but that Dunning had already figured in. Dealing with him was just the cost of doing business. The cost of the rum Dunning had paid Harris for in advance was trifling in comparison for what monies the high-quality deer skins and elk hides would bring at the Philadelphia fur market. Perhaps, Dunning pondered, he would have enough to forgo these dangerous trips and settle down to a trading post in the mountains along the south Allegheny path; close to the Warrior's Path would be a good spot he reckoned. Now all that mattered was the arduous and monotonous trip back up the Ohio. As they had left before having a chance to hunt or trade for food, Dunning knew that they would need to stop ahead, once they got past the Scioto and the last potential danger, Chartier.

Almost ten days of paddling had gone by since leaving the Miamis downriver, with consequence. The Shawnee village was passed without incident during the night, and in fact, Dunning and the men had not seen Indians on the river since then. However, the most pressing need now was to stop and hunt. The provisions of salt pork and dried corn purchased from Shannopin were gone, and the men were exhausted when they caught sight of the familiar island in the Ohio. Dunning remembered the deer and elk he and Hendricks had seen on the island from the channel of the river. Pointing to the Indian camp on the east shore, Dunning told McAfee, Quinn, and Smyth to paddle over there to the creek bank where the Indians had beached their canoes, and wait for him and Hendricks to meet them. They were going to kill a deer or two, quarter them, and bring the meat over, where he hoped they could all have something to eat with the Indians, at their camp, who were most likely, friendly Delaware of Shannopin's. Then Dunning and Hendricks paddled to the west channel of the Ohio, and soon out of sight of the other men, who worked their way over to the mouth of the creek and stopped at the overturned Indian canoes. A few Indian children who were playing on the creek bank curiously took notice of the three traders lounging in the canoe, sunning themselves. Quinn took out the last of his share of rum and drank it, as one of the women at the drying racks came over to see what the children were squawking about. Soon, all the women were aware of the presence of the white traders and sent one of the young girls up the trail to find the men and tell them to come.

McAfee, who knew the Lenape tongue, let the Smyth and Quinn know that the Indians were not Delaware, but Iroquois. McAfee, who understood enough of their language, called them Mingos, and remarked that they were probably from a village up the river close to Logstown. However, it was then that the three caught the irresistible smell of cooking food. Leaving the two guns in the canoe, Quinn and Smyth sauntered over to the nearby fire on the other side of the enormous elm tree next to the trail. McAfee lagged behind. The women called the children and young girls together and told them to go to the woods immediately. Smyth gestured to the Indian women by pointing to the pot and putting his hand to his mouth that he would like something to eat, but Shakes-Her-Fist waved her arm at them and pointed to their canoe, implying to everyone present that the whites should leave, and leave now with no food. Smyth gestured again, rubbing his stomach to imply that they were hungry, but to no avail. Shakes-Her-Fist would have none of it, and spoke angrily in the Iroquois tongue for the white men to leave. McAfee tried to call Smyth and Quinn back, reminding them that Dunning would be here soon anyway, and they could all eat then. However, Quinn was not listening, nor interested in food at the moment. He had had his eyes on a young Indian squaw next to Shakes-Her-Fist from the moment he set eyes on her. To Quinn, she appeared as if she was interested in him, or so he thought. Dunning was no longer around to keep his leash on him, and prevent him from having a little fun, Quinn rationalized. He spoke to the woman in English, telling her what a pretty young squaw she was, which none of the Indian women understood, least of all her. But Shakes-Her-Fist knew what the unmistakable glint in Quinn's eyes meant. Suddenly without warning, Quinn grabbed the Indian girl by the hand and pulled her away in the direction of one of the lean-tos to satisfy his hot blood, which was now up.

The woman screamed at the top of her lungs as Quinn threw her to the ground and began to lift up her blanket skirt to mount her. Shakes-Her-Fist ran to her aid, and grabbing a knot of wood next to the cooking fire and swung it at Quinn, catching him squarely on the side of his head, and breaking his jawbone in the process. Quinn howled in pain and reached for his knife. McAfee attempted to pull Quinn off the struggling half-naked woman beneath him just as Shakes-Her-Fist was getting ready to strike Quinn again. Enraged, Quinn caught Shakes-Her-Fist's left arm with his free hand and buried the blade of his knife into her ribcage beneath the arm pit, severing an internal artery, and stopping her in mid-stride. Stunned, and skewered by Quinn's knife, Shakes-Her-Fist fell to her knees as one of the women caught her. A smirk of satisfaction came over Quinn's leering face; his dark eyes darting back and forth between the bleeding woman and the young squaw whom he lusted for, who had broken free from him.

Just then, Little Skunk and his cousin barreled out of the woods and into the camp clearing, with guns in hand, screaming the war whoop. Pulling his knife out of Shakes-Her-Fist, Quinn ducked the shot that was sure to come from Little Skunk who had already put the musket to his cheek. The firelock roared, missing Quinn but hitting McAfee squarely in the upper chest, knocking him off his feet. On the other side of the island in the west channel of the Ohio River, Dunning and Hendricks looked up at each other and realized instantly that the shot following the unmistakable Indian war whoop could only mean trouble at the hunting camp. Dropping everything except their guns, they began to paddle furiously upriver to clear the island and make their way back downstream to the mouth of the creek. At the camp, Thomas Smyth who had just witnessed what had transpired, put his hands up in the air and waved at the warriors. He showed them that he had no weapons and tried to convince the Indians rushing towards him that had no part in what had happened, which was, in fact, the truth. It was to no avail. Little Skunk's cousin fired his gun at Smyth, catching him in the lower leg, and breaking both bones. Smyth was knocked head over heels and attempted to shimmy his way to the canoe without success, as the Indians were moments away from catching up with him. Quinn, with Shakes-Her-Fist's blood dripping from his hands, sized the situation up immediately and realized that the warriors were a hairs-breadth from getting him too. He made a run to the river, passing McAfee who was now laying at the water's edge, begging him for God's sake to help him. Quinn, oblivious to McAfee's plea, looked over his shoulder to see how close his pursuers were, and then leaped into the Ohio River and swan out into the current. One of the warriors leveled his musket and fired from shore, missing Quinn. In a few moments, Dunning and Hendricks appeared. They came downriver far enough out of musket range and waited for Quinn to swim out to them. They dragged him breathless into the canoe, whereupon the three of them began paddling upriver in haste. Asking Quinn where McAfee, Smyth and the other canoe with the skins were, Dunning was shocked when Quinn gasped, "We was attacked by them Injuns….the others are gone….all gone!"

Back in the camp, Little Skunk held Shakes-Her-Fist's head up as she lay where she had fallen. Her eyes, now fluttering, were glazing over. Bubbles of blood sputtered from her lips, as her chest labored to breathe. Little Skunk could see that she was dying, and with her, his child. She said only a few words to him as she lay there with her eyes now wide open, gazing up, in her final moments of life. "I see the Tree of my dreams," she said to Little Skunk, referring to the big elm whose limbs was spread out against the sky above her, appearing just as she had seen in her dreams as a child. "It is my Death… It has come for me and our son….I go now and take the little one with me." And as she died, Little Skunk could feel the infant in her belly struggle and kick for the life that was not to be. In anguish, Little Skunk let out a long agonizing scream that even Dunning could hear, now more than a quarter mile away. Shakes-Her-Fist and her child were gone; dead, and Little Skunk was inconsolable in grief. A hundred feet away, Little Skunk's cousin reached the unfortunate John McAfee, who was seriously wounded. Carefully cutting open the white man's clothing off him, the Indian inserted his knife blade into McAfee's lower belly, and began cutting open the intestinal cavity up to his breastbone, after first cutting Moran's genitals off and putting them in front of his open eyes. Then giving McAfee's open belly a jerk with his knife, he disemboweled him, kicking the steaming guts into the river with disgust. McAfee's mouth moved as if he were trying to speak, but nothing came out. Little Skunk's cousin was not done. He expertly cut off the man's nose and ears before running his knife around the crown of his head, and jerking off the scalp with a popping sound. He finished by chopping McAfee's skunk open with his hatchet, and then hacking the body into pieces. Finally, Little Skunk's cousin kicked the stinking, bloody mess that had once been a human being into the river before returning to Little Skunk and the others, with the bloody scalp of John McAfee in his sash belt. One piece of vengeance had been fulfilled.

There was silence in the hunting camp except for two sounds; that of a mourning wail from Little Skunk as he laid his head upon the belly of Shakes-Her-Fist, and the painful howl coming from Thomas Smyth whose leg was broken in two places. Finally, after more than an hour, Little Skunk raised his head and sat up, staring in the direction of Smyth. A look of complete utter hatred filled his eyes. The barely-controlled rage rising within him emanated from a pit of emptiness that was his entire being. Nothing would ever again fill his life with happiness or contentment as he once had felt. It was if he had died inside—that he was as if already dead, but still present among the living. Little Skunk walked over to Smyth, who could not stand, and stepped hard on the man's broken leg, causing the shattered bone to break the skin. Smyth screamed in pain, but unfortunately for him, his long painful ordeal was only beginning. Little Skunk took his time preparing for it. He stripped Smyth naked and painted his face black, indicating that the man was condemned to death in retribution for Little Skunk's grievous loss. It did not matter to him in the least which one of the whites was responsible, nor did he ask. Shakes-Her-Fist and his son yet to be born were dead, and Smyth had been there when it happened. Vengeance must be taken and fulfilled for the sake of Shakes-Her-Fist, for Little

Skunk's unborn son, and to cleanse the evil that had happened to his family and that now laid upon his own shoulders. Little Skunk would see to it that vengeance would be fulfilled and that this place of evil white men would never be forgotten.

Smyth was tied to the big tree with several leather thongs around his torso and at his knees, forcing him to stand on his badly shattered leg. Then Little Skunk kindled a small fire around Smyth's bare feet. Soon Smyth's flesh began hissing as it roasted. Smyth screamed at the top of his lungs at the unbearable unrelenting pain, but Little Skunk was unmoved among the group of men and boys seated in a semi-circle around Smyth. Hour by hour, Little Skunk fed the fire at Smyth's feet until it was evident that his feet had been entirely consumed by the flames, leaving only blackened bones hanging from his leg stumps. When Smyth lost consciousness from the pain, Little Skunk let up, pouring water over Smyth's head to revive him. Then Little Skunk would continue. Next he placed red hot iron tools, his musket barrel, and hatchet head to Smyth's bare body, causing renewed shrieks from Smyth who was still alive. The other men joined in and the boys as well in burning Smyth with anything they could find, including hickory poles lit at one end which burned exceedingly hot. They poked Smyth until every inch of the skin on his body below his neck had been blackened and charred. Still, Little Skunk's vengeance was not complete. He cut off Smyth's ears, nose and eyelids until the face was unrecognizable. What was left of the man who had once been Thomas Smyth begged for death and an end to his suffering, but none was forthcoming until Little Skunk's fury had been sated. Finally, after two days Little Skunk could see that the time had come to end this. He sliced off Smyth's scalp before opening his lower body cavity and allowing Smyth's intestines to drop onto the fiery coals below where they hissed and smoked. Then, as a last act, Little Skunk cut Smyth down and severed his head from the torso with his hatchet. What was left of the unrecognizable human body was thrown into the Ohio River, but the head was kept separate, so that his spirit would roam the afterlife and find no peace. Wordlessly, Little Skunk worked into the night fashioning a pointed twelve foot pole which he stood upright and buried an end into the ground in the center of the camp. On the other end, Little Skunk placed the scalped, mutilated head of Thomas Smyth, as evidence that vengeance had been fulfilled at this place of a white man's evil. No one with him would ever forget. It was a place which had already been named by Little Skunk's family, spoken in Iroquois as, "Kanororan—Place of the Skull, a Place of White Man's Evil."

Little Skunk's life was forever changed. He would live his life to its end, never forgetting that fateful day when his wife and child perished at the hands of the evil white men. Knowing that flesh had been paid for with flesh, and life with life was little consolation for the bitter loss he felt. Place of the Skull would never again serve as a hunting camp, but rather, a place where vengeance had been delivered for the grievous act of the murder of an Indian woman and her unborn baby by a white man, that would never be forgotten. As to the murderer of Shakes-Her-Fist, John Quinn never spoke of it to Dunning, Hendricks, or anyone else till the day he died. A man with no conscience to bother him, Quinn would go to his grave with the secret that only he knew, or remembered in sober moments, which were very few. But no grave would Quinn find to rest in death, either. The Okton waiting in the spirit world for Quinn's soul would see to that. On Conrad Weiser's trip across the northern Allegheny trail for a council to be held with the

Indians at Logstown, Pennsylvania's ambassador to the Indians noted in his journal on the 24th of August, 1748: "Found a Dead Man on the Road who had killed himself by Drinking too much Whiskey; the Place being very stony we could not dig a Grave—He smelling very strong we covered him with Stones and Wood and went on our Journey. " Then on the return trip home to Pennsylvania in September, Conrad made an entry that read: "The 22nd, the weather cleared up; we travelled this day about 35 miles, came by the place where we had buried the body of John Quen, but found the bears had pulled him out and left nothing of him but a few naked bones and some old rags…" [81]

Place of the Skull

Part 3: Why

Place of the Skull

Chapter 9: Reasons found in the Spirit World

The question why a white man's head was placed upon a pole was never adequately asked or answered by the first settlers of the colonial frontier who entered the Indian lands of the Ohio Country in the late 1760's. They heard of the creek named by the Indians, the Place of the Skull. But who was the white man whose head was severed and put up on a pole at the mouth of the creek flowing into the Ohio River? Why was this done and for what reason? If the answer to the question of who was not known, the answer to why was known without any doubt. Every white man on the frontier knew why—it was simply an act of Indian savagery. There was no need to understand more about why the Indians placed a white man's head on a pole beyond that answer. Indians were savages. They committed savage despicable acts, and this was one of them. To gain a deeper insight into the Indian state of mind that shaped their actions was fruitless, and unnecessary. The two minds—the native American Woodland Indian and the white Judeo-Christian European—had rarely shared rapport on any level since the entrance of Europeans to the continent. Simply put, Indians and whites looked upon each other from either side of an immense gulf of misunderstanding and mistrust. Neither could begin to understand the other, much less find a level of rapport beyond the manner in which their culture had shaped their thinking. At the heart of it was an ingrained racist view from the white, European perspective that all Indians were racially, culturally, and spiritually inferior. As such, Indians should be totally subjugated, assimilated into white culture, or exterminated if they resisted.

Through the eyes of most 18th Century white Christian Europeans living on the frontier, Indians were considered barbaric, savage, pagan peoples with few redeeming qualities even when they were converted to Christianity. This was due to their basic inferior nature that was evident, when compared to white people, by their red-brown skin color. Too, their lack of cities, roads, written language, formal education, Christian religion, government, manufacturing, and judicial system based upon ethics and morals was lacking; thus a testament to their primitiveness and inferiority. Simply understood, Indians had not as yet invented the wheel; an ancient invention of the Egyptians, Hittites and Greeks. How could they then be viewed as anything but savages bred from an unforgiving forest wilderness? These were not ideas debated upon in New York and Philadelphia. They were understood as given facts by all colonials. Indians were a product of their environment; a primitive culture that had not evolved in the same manner as European culture. As such, it was comprehensible to white society that savages such as the American Woodland Indian were capable of savagery because it was their very nature. It was what Indians were about. The derisive words used by white European traders and settlers on the frontier to describe Indians attests to that implicit understanding. Indians were viewed by whites as red-skinned cruel barbarians. John Heckewelder, who ministered to the Indians during most of his lifetime knew Indian nature very well and balked at the prevailing attitude. Heckewelder wrote of the prevalent white attitude of 18th Century, "They (Indians) must of course be barbarians and savages; by which undefined words is understood whatever is bad, wicked, and disgraceful to human nature....A species of monsters, to whom cruelty is an appetite; a sort of human-shaped tigers and panthers, strangers to the finer feelings, and who commit acts of barbarity without any excitement but that of their depraved inclination." [82]

However, Heckewelder believed that this white attitude towards Indians was far from the truth, and nothing less than an unjust racial bias against them. "Unless Indians were consistently provoked into retaliation or revenge, they were of noble and great character." [83] Conrad Weiser agreed. He had lived among the Mohawk for years, before becoming Pennsylvania's emissary to the Iroquois League. Conrad found them gentle—as long as the rum trader was absent, saying, "One can be among them for thirty years and more and never once see two sober Indians fight or quarrel." [84] Yet the racial stereotype of Indians persisted. Names given to Indians reflected the attitude of hatred towards them. Indians were red devils, red niggars, and vermin. This was because if you were one of those white men on the frontier who had seen the handiwork of Indians during times of war, Indians were a raced to be exterminated, and cleansed from the land by any means possible. Obviously, white people found Indians a hindrance to the acquisition of their land which lay waiting for civilized settlement. The Indians were well aware of the desire of white people to take Indian land by any means. Explained Heckewelder, Indians found whites "an ungrateful, insatiable people, who, though the Indians had given them as much land as was necessary to raise provisions for themselves and their families, wanted still to have more, and at last would not be contented with less than the *whole country*." Said an Iroquois Indian to Weiser in 1737, "Time will show what is to happen to us; rum will kill us, and leave the land clear for the Europeans, without strife or purchase." [85] Yet more than a hundred years later, the attitude still persisted. General Sheridan, at a council with the

Comanche in Oklahoma Territory in January 1869, made a remark that summed up the continuation of the white man's hatred and prejudice for Indians when he said, "The only good Indian I ever saw was a dead Indian." [86]

So for an Indian to kill a white man, cut off his head, and then place it at the top of a post was understood by whites as nothing more than a random act of brutality committed by a savage people. During times of war, colonials had seen the extent of bloody savagery that Indians were capable of committing upon whites. Indians did not fight like white European soldiers, who stood out in the open in lines and fired their guns at each other. Indians were considered by whites to fight in a cowardly manner from ambush. They attacked their unsuspecting enemy, hurled themselves upon them, and then fled into the forests before they could be pursued. Indians routinely tore the bodies of their dead victims open and disemboweled, mutilated, and cut off the scalp on the head. White women and children were not always considered by Indians to be non-combatants in war; they could be just as easily slain or mistreated as white males. Worst of all, Indians were known to ritually torture and burn to death their male prisoners in a most horrible, despicable, and inhuman manner that shocked white sensibilities. The burning of prisoners reinforced white sentiments that the best policy governing relations with the Indians should be their complete destruction. Of course, whites overlooked their own savage treatment of Indians on the frontier when it was called upon. Heckewelder attests to scores of outrages perpetrated upon Delaware Indians in Pennsylvania and the Ohio Country by whites. When whites murdered peaceful Indians, Heckewelder noted that the Indians had, "no prospect of obtaining redress themselves for the wrongs they had suffered." [87] No colonial court could arrest and convict a white man of murdering an Indian. Whites, on the other hand, rationalized their own brutality against Indians as a necessary evil in dealing with evil; invoking the Biblical proverb of the Old Testament of "An eye for an eye and a tooth for a tooth," [88] against "beasts of prey in the human form; men with whom no faith is to be kept, and who ought to be cut off from the face of the earth!" [89]

If placing a severed white man's head upon a post was a random act of Indian savagery, there is no evidence in colonial records to show that it was a common practice. Instead, it was uncommonly rare. More compelling is the question of why Indians would take notice of a random act of violence against a white man if it was nothing out of the ordinary. Why call the locale of a random act of violence the Place of the Skull if it was just one in hundreds upon hundreds of random acts of Indian savagery? If it was random, then naming the place of a random act seems unlikely. On the other hand, if it was natural for Indians to name places of random acts of savagery, why do the colonial records not bear that out? Why has the site of Place of the Skull, not come up elsewhere? Why are there no place names east of the Mississippi River from the 18th Century noted in records as Indian names for Place of the Scalped Prisoner, Place of the Burned White Man, and Place of the Disemboweled Body? None exist. Nowhere else in America is there a place named by 18th Century Indians as Place of the Skull. It can only mean that the white men of that day misinterpreted the act as meaningless, and settled with that explanation when, in fact, it was not random and not meaningless.

Placing a white man's head on a post was very meaningful to the Indians who did it. It had great significance to them, or they would have disposed of the head along with the body, not giving it a thought more than the effort it took to cut the victim's scalp off before they left. To sever a dead man's head takes a great deal of effort using 18th Century hand tools that Indians carried with them—the hatchet and the scalping knife. It would take time to cut through the flesh of the neck, severing arteries, muscles and ligaments. Cutting or chopping through the upper neck vertebrae is no easy feat. Once complete, the head, with the remains of the vertebrae still attach inside the cranium, has to be mounted on the sharpened end of a stick or pole. It would not automatically slide into the skull. The end of the pole needed to be carefully sharpened to a long narrow point, which would take time and skill using hand tools. In addition, a hole would need to be made into the base of the skull for the wood to insert internally, or the skull would fall off, considering that the whole effort was done so as to have the head remain mounted for a period of time. Excess vertebrae and ligament and muscle tissue would need cut away. In short, putting a head on a post was nothing less than a time-consuming labor making the project not a random act of savagery, but an act done with a specific purpose in mind.

Some 18th Century settlers to the area, and later historians as well, came to the conclusion that the Indians placed the white man's head upon a post as a warning. This idea resulted from some Delaware Indians telling John Heckewelder, Moravian minister to the Indians, that, "the Indians [Delaware] said that they had decapitated a prisoner and placed his head upon a pole," during one of their previous wars. [90] Hence the Delaware word for head, "Wihl" with the locative, "ing" meant "place of the head," which together Wihl-ing or Wheeling, gave the name to the creek. Allegedly, the severed head was placed upon a pole facing the river as a warning to future intruders to stay out of Delaware land.

The Zane brothers, Ebenezer, Jonathan and Silas, were the first settlers to arrive at the mouth of the creek in September 1769 from crossing the Alleghenies. It was reported years later that Ebenezer said that they had met an old Delaware Indian near the site who told them that the creek was named Place of the Skull, in the Delaware language. Thus the Zanes added credence to the claim by local Indians, and so the name became commonly used by the white settlers arriving in the area after the Zanes. However, there are problems with this claim made by the Delaware.

The Delaware, in fact, were not the originators of the name. When the French officer and diplomat Celeron de Blainville came down the Ohio River on an expedition from Canada to lay claim to the lands drained by the Ohio River and its tributaries for France in the summer of 1749, the creek was already named by the Iroquois. Celeron had Iroquois Indians accompanying him on the voyage down the Ohio. The Iroquois knew the name of the creek by the name "Kanonuara" as spelled phonetically in Celeron's journal, [91] which translates in the Iroquoian language into Place of the Head or Skull. Celeron stated, "The next day, August 13th 'at noon I (Celeron) made a halt and had a leaden plate buried at the entrance of the River Kanonuara, to the south of the Beautiful River," after leaving Logstown. [92] Another journal of the expedition was kept by Father Joseph Pierre de Bonnecamps. He referred to the same creek. "I will only tell you that we buried three plates of lead at the mouths of three different rivers, the 1st of which was called Kanonouaora....[Bonnecamps spelling.]" [93] In addition to his journal entry, Bonnecamps included a map which places Kanonouaora as in the correct coordinates as Wheeling Creek in relation to the creeks and villages previously visited. Several things can be deduced from this.

First, David Zeisberger, Moravian preacher to the Delaware and associate of John Heckewelder, notes in his Indian Dictionary, that the Iroquois Onondaga word for 'Head' is "Anuwara" which translates into the Delaware language as "Wihl, or Wilunk," meaning Place of the Head. [94] This means that the Delaware, who were not present in the Wheeling Creek area until years later, learned the word-name for the creek, from the Iroquois. Secondly, the Iroquois accompanying the Celeron expedition were already aware of the name of the creek and its meaning, and so recommended to Celeron that a lead plate be buried there because of the significance of the site to the Iroquois. It could have been buried at the mouth of what is now Short Creek above Wheeling Creek or at the mouth of Grave Creek which is just below Wheeling Creek, both of which are relatively the same size, but it was not. Celeron, who had never been down the Ohio, had no reference to go by as to where to bury his lead plates. He relied upon the advice of the Iroquois travelling with him, and they decided upon the site of what is now Wheeling Creek. The Iroquois already knew of the major east-west Indian path that crossed the Ohio River at the mouth of Wheeling Creek, but more importantly, the event surrounding the name of the creek held special significance to them, and them alone, and not to the Delaware. This is because the event that had transpired at the mouth of the creek years prior to Celeron's arrival **had involved Iroquois Indians** and a white man, and not anyone else. [95] This means that the Delaware, at some time prior to telling their story to both Heckewelder and the Zanes, had translated the Iroquois word into their own language, or substituted one for the other. The place-name was correct but the details of what happened were wrong, due to the amount of time that had passed since the actual event which occurred prior to Celeron's visit to Wheeling Creek in 1749 to bury a lead plate for France's land claim.

Something else is interesting about this. Both Celeron and Bonnecamps kept detailed records of their stops and camps during the trip down the Ohio River, giving much valuable background information at each place. Why then did neither of them record the discovery of a skull mounted upon a pole on the north bank of Wheeling Creek? Especially with a name place describing the head or skull of a white man it would be thought that either one of these two men would have noted such a significant find. The explanation is two-fold. First, no skull was found by anyone of Celeron's entourage during their stop on the north bank of the creek. This is because the skull had already deteriorated and fallen to the ground, and covered with a succession of autumn leaves until the bone parts were entirely dissolved. This would have occurred after a maximum period of up to five years that it takes for a skull to decay, but no longer than that. Weather, insects, sunlight, and winter freeze and thaw would have destroyed the remains of the skull. The pole would have rotted off and fallen in that same period, if not sooner. This places the event of the killing of the white victim and the erection of the pole with his head on it, at least five years prior to Celeron's visit, or to be exact, 1744 or 1745. By the time Celeron arrived, the evidence was gone, but the name had not.

The creek had already been named by the Iroquois at the time of the event; thus the Indians with Celeron knew in advance where the creek was, what the name of it was, and what had transpired there. However, the Iroquois gave Celeron and Bonnecamps the name of the creek, but not the meaning of the word, nor did they explain to the Frenchman what had happened there. That is why there is no mention of the translation of what *Kanonuara* or the word *Anuwara* meant in either French man's journal. The Iroquois had a reason they did not want either man to know because they knew that the place was known to the Iroquois as a place of white man's evil. Almost two years later, in 1751, Christopher Gist, a frontier scout and trader, was sent on a mission by the newly-formed Ohio Company of Virginia to survey the lands on the east and south side of the Ohio River from the mouth of the Kanawha River north. Gist was unaware of the visit by Celeron and the French in 1749, and the buried lead plates claiming the land for France. However, Gist, in the company of his son, and an unnamed Indian scout reached the mouth of "a Creek called Wealin or Scalp Creek where we encamped," [96] on Saturday March 7th 1751. Apparently Gist's unnamed Indian scout was Delaware, says Norona. "It indicates that the tragedy occurred before Celeron's expedition of 1749, and that the atrocity was probably committed by Iroquois Indians." [97] From the Delaware scout Gist employed, he learned the name of the creek in question, as Gist had no previous knowledge of it. On Sunday, Gist explored up the creek now called Wheeling Creek. "We went out to search the Land which We found very good for near 15 M up this Creek from the Mouth of it, the Bottoms about a mile wide and some Meadows—We found an old Indian Road up this Creek," [98] referring to the ancient east-west Indian path later called the Mingo Path.

Why were the Delaware correct about the name of the creek derived from the Iroquois but incorrect about claiming the act of putting a white man's head up on a post was a warning to white settlers? First, the Delaware did not live in the Ohio Country lands below Logstown prior to 1749, and even later than that. Celeron found no Indians living at Wheeling Creek.

Secondly, the Delaware had no claim to the land which was Iroquois land by rights of conquest, thus it was not in their power to tell anyone to stay out of the land. Additionally, there was no war between whites and any Indians living in the Ohio Country prior to 1749. The French and Indian War that would result partially from Celeron's land claim would not begin until 1755. Most important of all in disputing the Delaware claim, is that there were no white English or French settlers coming into the lands of the Ohio Country, much less the Wheeling Creek area. During this time period, absolutely none were to be found. None were travelling down the Ohio River. The Zanes, the first English settlers to the area, would not make their appearance until twenty years after Celeron. Since the creek was already named by the Iroquois prior to 1749, there were no settlers for the Delaware to base their claim upon. Therefore, they were incorrect in claiming that the head or skull on a pole was put there as a warning to whites.

Woodland Indians had no means of recording stories and events with a written language, and therefore depended upon traditional oral history of telling a story of an event that would be retold over and over through time. The Delaware, who were aware of the creek by its name, did not have the correct details of the story, as would have been told by the Iroquois to them who obviously knew what happened prior to 1749. The Delaware claim that the reason a white man's head was severed and put upon on a post as a warning to interlopers was simply not true. The Delaware were not there at the time of the incident. They had only heard about what happened from other Indians who had heard about it from the Iroquois, and by 1769, twenty-five years had passed in the interim between the actual event and it being told to the Zanes. The details were blurred, forgotten, or never told to the specific Delaware who told the story to Heckewelder and the Zanes. Since the Delaware had no written language to quote from, it was related to Zane from a story told over and over for twenty-five years and from one generation to another that the specific Indians were quoting from memory. That the Zanes and others adopted the Delaware explanation is understandable. It could be easily explained as another act of random Indian savagery with a warning attached. However, this is not the case. The colonial historical record has virtually no instances of severed heads put up on poles by the Indians as a warning.

Some white settlers and later historians came to believe that the story of the Indians putting a white man's head on a pole at Wheeling meant that the Indians were simply displaying the victim's head as a trophy after killing him. This belief was erroneous for several reasons. The colonial historical records, including diaries and logs of prominent white men of the 18th Century who were emissaries or liaisons to the many Woodland tribes of the northeast, make rare reference to any head-on-a-pole incidents. Men like George Croghan, Conrad Weiser, William Johnson, John Heckewelder and David Zeisberger, due to their close proximity to the Indian tribes and their constant interaction with them through the French and Indian War period, Pontiac's Rebellion, and the American Revolution, would surely have noted the trophy taking of victim's heads if it was a common practice. In fact, it was extremely rare. It was noted that when the British force commanded by General Forbes succeeded in taking the French Fort Duquesne at the Forks of the Ohio in late 1758, they found many mens' heads mounted on poles taken from the dead of Grant's Highlanders. "As they neared the fort, the Highlanders were goaded to fury at seeing the heads of their slaughtered comrades stuck on poles, round which the kilts were hung derisively, in imitation of petticoats." [99] The heads on poles were found in the abandoned French-allied Indian camp outside the walls of the fort, placed there as trophies brought back to camp to be displays of the Indian's decisive victory over Grant's Highlanders on Grant's Hill, several miles east of Fort Duquesne.

As such, the displaying of the heads of enemies on poles as trophies, though rare, was always performed in the Indian camp for all of the tribe to observe and admire the destruction of an enemy individual, just as scalp posts were erected in Indian villages for display. Major Robert Rogers noted scalp trophies taken by the Indians when his rangers destroyed the French-allied Abenaki village of St. Francis in a surprise raid in September 1759. "Upon entering the village, Roger's men saw some six or seven hundred English scalps; wafting in the wind, they hung from poles erected over doors of the houses and atop other prominent buildings." [100] Coincidentally, no heads or skulls on poles were found. An instance was recorded during the American Revolution, in the spring of 1779, in Ohio Country. Captain Bird, of the King's Eighth British Regiment was sent from Fort Detroit to the Upper Sandusky Indian villages to prepare for a combined Indian and British force to attack the American post of Fort Laurens. Arriving at the Wyandot Indian town, Bird found a group of warriors preparing to torture a white Virginian militiaman captured from the vicinity of Fort Laurens. Bird tried to intervene to save the man's life, to no avail, as the Indians "cut the man's throat and 'murdered him at a most horrid rate." When the Wyandots were finished dismembering the corpse, Captain Bird had some of his men bury the body only to find that the Indians soon dug it up and put the scalped head upon a pole and raised it in the center of the village." [101] Again, as seen in this case, the head of the victim was placed upon the pole in the center of the village as a display of an enemy trophy for all to see. But to say that putting a victim's head on a pole at a spot in the wilderness, where no other Indian would see it to appreciate it as a trophy, is not the case. There are other more plausible reasons to consider.

Vengeance is the act of seeking revenge against another party by a counterblow or settling a score against them for a wrong or perceived wrong. To 18th Century Woodland Indians, like most tribal peoples around the world, seeking and fulfilling vengeance ranked high, if not highest, in the motivation of individuals, families, clans and tribes. Seeking vengeance led to wars between Indians, as in the case of the Iroquois and Catawba, and the Iroquois and the Huron, prior to the introduction of Europeans to America. However small the score may be that needed settled, such as another tribe's hunting party trespassing on one's own lands, it nevertheless needed avenging, regardless of the cost. Heckewelder, who was fond of native people in America, ranked vengeance as their greatest weakness, with alcoholism second. Said Heckewelder in summing up Indian character in general, "The worst that can be said of them is, that the passion of revenge is so **strong in their minds**, that it carries them beyond all bounds....I admit that the Indians have sometimes revenged, cruelly revenged, the accumulated wrongs which they have suffered from unprincipled white men; the love of revenge is a strong passion which their imperfect religious notions have not taught them to subdue." [102] Indians were known to go to great lengths seeking revenge, especially when murder of one of their own was involved and the grievous harm done to them was greatest. A case in point is the burning at the stake of Colonel William Crawford by the Delaware in June, 1782, during the American Revolution. Months previous, an expedition of American militiamen had massacred ninety-six unarmed Christian Delaware Indians at the Moravian mission of Gnadenhutten in the Ohio Country. The mounted militia force had been led by Colonel David Williamson. In June, Crawford and Williamson set out with some 500 mounted militiamen for the Upper Sandusky Indian villages to attack them. Unexpectedly, they were attacked first by Indians and British Rangers and subsequently defeated. Williamson and some of the militiamen escaped but Crawford was captured, along with a handful of men.

As the story was related to Heckewelder, it was decided by the Delaware that all the captives would be put to death to fulfill vengeance against their dead relatives at Gnadenhutten. Crawford, who knew the Delaware war chief, Captain Wingemund, from their days at Fort Pitt before the war, spoke to him before he was to be burned alive. Crawford explained to Wingemund that it was not him who was responsible for the Moravian Massacre, but Williamson. The Delaware chief agreed that that was so, but explained to Crawford that the Delaware, knowing that Williamson had escaped, "They have taken you, they will take revenge on you in his stead." Crawford pleaded with his old friend to save him, but begrudgingly, Wingemund told him, "I tell you with grief. Had Williamson been taken [prisoner] with you, I and some friends, by making use of what you have told me, might perhaps, have succeeded to save you, but as the matter now stands, no man would dare to interfere in your behalf. The King of England himself, were he to come to this spot, with all his wealth and treasures could not affect this purpose. The blood of the innocent Moravians, more than half of them women and children, cruelly and wantonly murdered calls aloud for *revenge*. The relatives of the slain, who are amongst us, cry out and stand ready for

151

revenge. The nation to which they belonged will have *revenge*. The Shawanese, our grandchildren, have asked for your fellow-prisoner [Dr. Knight;] [103] on him they will take revenge. All the nations connected with us cry out *Revenge! Revenge!* The Moravians whom you went to destroy have fled, instead of avenging their brethren, the offence is become national, and the nation itself is bound to take REVENGE!" [104]

Revenge for a grievous act, such as murder committed against one or more of their own people was a primary motivating factor, but not the only one, that caused the Iroquois to kill their prisoner and place his head upon a pole at Wheeling Creek. This was not the case of a stray white trader that the Iroquois came upon and killed for no reason. The white man in question had committed a grievous act against the Indians, and that act had to be none other than a heinous murder of innocent Indians, meaning women and children. To Indians, the more heinous the act committed against them, the greater the level of retaliation was needed to fulfill vengeance and right the wrong. In this case, as the story has been told of one white man as the victim, it is easy to see through Iroquois eyes that the one white man had done something despicable that warranted severing his head, after a more than likely gruesome death, as suggested by the Narrative. But if revenge was all important to the Iroquois, why did not killing the white man alone warrant vengeance fulfilled? Why did they have to sever his head and put in up on a pole if it wasn't a random act of savagery, a warning to others, or a misplaced trophy? Crawford's head was not severed and put up on a pole in the center of the Delaware village for all to see and relish in vengeance fulfilled. No, something else was at work in the minds of the Iroquois who took revenge on the white man who had committed murder against one of their family. It is not enough to say then that the head on a pole at the mouth of Wheeling Creek was simply a display of vengeance fulfilled by the family of the murdered Indian, which it was. Something more is needed to understand what happened.

Is it not enough to say that the Iroquois Indian who put the severed head of the white man on a pole was doing it solely for himself as a statement affirming his fulfillment of vengeance? If so, then was his display for no one else's benefit that his own? It would make for more sense that his display was symbolic and only the outward manifestation of something going on in his own mind. He would have shared no illusion that the outward manifestation, the head on the post, would not last long, and would rapidly deteriorate until the skull fell apart. But if that act was symbolic only to him, and had an inward meaning in his own mind not understandable in the outer world, then what was he was trying to accomplish? Woodland Indian religion across tribes held as a basic principle that "Spirit was the prime reality. All things had souls: not only man, but also animals, the air, water, trees, even rocks and stones," created by the "Great Spirit, the Creator," states Paul Wallace. [105] Wrote David Zeisberger, "They believe and have from time immemorial believed that there is an Almighty Being who has created heaven and earth and man and all things else," [106] added that "They consider the soul to be an invisible being and a spirit." [107] However, in this manifest world created by the Great Spirit also reside "certain spirit forces on earth," including evil spirits. Consequently, the manifest world of the Woodland Indian was a spirit world, "which was alive and visible in every aspect of nature," [108] contrary to the religion of Christianity that Europeans brought with them to America. The fact that Indians like the Iroquois did not have a written body of religious doctrine and cosmology does not mean that they did not carry with them a spirit religion inside their mind, or a religious mentality. Their religious view of a spirit world that they dwelt in was summed up by a Shawnee chief who told Count Zinzendorf in 1742, "The difference between the Indian's religion and the white man's religion was that the Indian had it in his heart while the white man had it on his lips," [109] meaning scripture and doctrine.

Within that Indian view of the spirit world was the unshakable conviction that the soul or spirit of a person survives death, and lingers close to the body for a period of time before making its sojourn to join the Great Spirit. "When a man died, his soul, though it immediately left the body, remained in the neighborhood for eleven days. On the twelfth, it set out on its twelve-year journey." [110] However, intentionally separating the head from the body at death could interrupt this transmigration of the spirit of the deceased, and cause it to wander the spirit world of the afterlife forever without peace. This was because the spirit of a person was believed to reside in the head; consequently it was important that precise burial rites be followed for a deceased Indian. When his body was interred, "The head was turned to the east and the feet to the west," wrote Zeisberger. [111] So severing the head of a person who had committed murder against one's family or friends was the ultimate act of revenge. By severing the head, and putting it up on a pole, the deceased person's spirit was damned to the spirit world of this plane, unable to transmigrate. "It was believed that if someone did not get the burial rites that were due upon death....their spirit was doomed to remain on the earthly plane....in a cycle that would cause unrest for the spirits." [112] This Indian belief was real to them, so the act of severing the head of the white man at Wheeling Creek served to damn his spirit as well as his body in death.

But most of important of all was the Woodland Indian belief that no events in the manifest world were unconnected from each other in the spirit world. To the Indian psyche, all things are spirit, holistically joined together in meaning, without distinctions or gradations. Consequently, a heinous evil act, like the murder of an innocent woman or child could only be understood as an act committed by an evil person without a distinction between the two. In turn, the evil in the white person was one and the same manifestation of an evil spirit in the spirit world inhabiting the body of the man who committed the act itself. Finally, the evil spirit, the evil man, and the evil act were all part of the same evil that inhabited the place or site where the act was committed. This would have been all the more understandable to the Iroquois because the murderer was none other than a white English man, a rum trader, who was considered by all Indians in the first half of the 18th Century as evil men possessed by evil spirits intent on debauching and destroying Indians with their liquor trade, to which they were helpless to resist or stop because of their weakness for white man's liquor.

"Native people believed themselves to be the primary victims of witchcraft. Devastating epidemics devastated Native populations, white encroachment depleted their game and took away their land, and periodic warfare brought violent death and turned Native worlds upside down," says Matthew Dennis in explaining the Indian view and belief that the white man brought with him more evil to the Indians than good since his appearance on the continent. [113] Holistically, to the Iroquois who had fulfilled vengeance, it was a white man's evil spirit that committed the act of murder, and at a white man's place of evil towards all Indians. Thus Wheeling Creek, by being so named as Place of the Skull, became recognized by all Indians of the Ohio

Country, and not just the Iroquois, as an evil place possessed by an evil spirit; in this case, of all that was bad and evil about white men. Ebenezer Zane, who settled at Wheeling Creek in 1769, knew nothing of the true Indian meaning of the creek's name as an evil white man's place. Ironically, Zane would become an embodiment of white man's evil during the American Revolution because he could not be killed or dislodged from the place that Indians viewed as white man's evil incarnate.

Weiser gives insight into the Indian's holistic view of the world in regards to evil acts, evil people, evil spirits and evil places all rolled into one. In the spring of 1736, the Pennsylvania government wished Conrad Weiser to go to Onondaga, the seat of the council of the Iroquois League, and deliver a message to them. Weiser agreed, and set out at once on February 27th with an Onondaga Iroquois Indian named Owisgera to guide him and his other companion Stoffel Stump over the Pennsylvania Mountains. Days later, several Iroquois joined Weiser on the trip. On March 26th Weiser noted that the Iroquois told him that they were entering a valley where "an Okton (an evil spirit) has power." [114] Explains Dennis, "Agotkon, utgon, or otkon, for the Iroquois, was an evil power or force" in the world that could inhabit both beings and places. [115] Weiser questioned the Indians about the evil spirit whom the Indians believed could be called by name and appeased with sacrifices, which they could not do without a magician. The next day, upon reaching the summit of the mountain, "We saw two skulls fixed on poles, the heads of men who had been killed there a long time before by their prisoners, who had been taken in South Carolina." [116] In this case, the skulls were of two Iroquois who had been killed by two Catawba prisoners, who were being taken north to the Iroquois villages to be burned, as was the custom between the two irresolute enemies. The prisoners had got loose during the overnight stay and killed their Iroquois captors. However, they had taken the time to sever the heads of the two Iroquois and place them on poles before returning south with the weapons of their former captives.

The Iroquois told Weiser that "The prisoners, [Catawba] who were two resolute men, had found themselves at night untied, which, without a doubt, had been done by the Okton," or evil spirit residing in the mountain. In this case, two Iroquois were the victims, and had their heads placed upon poles, neither as random acts of violence, or as trophies. While the two Catawba warriors used determination and ingenuity to untie themselves to escape, they paused long enough to kill their captors in an act of revenge, sever their heads and place them up on poles with great effort. Was this done to serve as a warning to future Iroquois? It seems hardly possible, as only Indians traveling to or from the Iroquois nations would pass along the path leading to the summit of the mountain. However, what is more likely is that the Catawba were aware of the Iroquois belief that the mountain held an evil spirit in the spirit world, and were in agreement with that belief, as their own tribe held similar beliefs about the spirit realm. Even if they untied themselves wholly on their own, by being aware that there was the presence of an evil spirit, they could easily rationalize that they had help in doing so, because it was no coincidence that they freed themselves at the locale of an evil spirit. They did not necessarily consider their enemy Iroquois captors as evil, but they did acknowledge that an evil spirit inhabiting the mountain was present and had a hand in what transpired. And therein lays the insight needed to understand fully the significance of placing the severed head on a pole when evil was present, such as what happened at Wheeling Creek.

In both cases, the Indians who committed the act of severing their enemy's heads did so partly out of revenge, but more out of symbolic sacrifice and protection. The Iroquois at Wheeling Creek recognized the presence of evil by the evil act committed by the white man, who was but an instrument for an evil spirit possessing him. Likewise the two Catawba warriors acknowledged the presence of an evil spirit, not in their Iroquois captors, but in the mountain that contained it, the spirit being the instrument used to allow for their escape. Killing the evil white man at Wheeling Creek satisfied the need for vengeance, however, severing his head and placing it upon a pole was the act of sacrificing the victim's spirit to the evil entity, thus affording the Indian who did so, a degree of psychic protection in the spirit world from both the evil spirit and the spirit of the deceased, who was now captivated or devoured by the evil spirit. In the case of the Catawba, severing the heads of the two Iroquois and placing them upon poles was a necessary sacrifice to the Otkon evil spirit. By giving or offering up the souls of the two dead Indians, in return, they believed they were granted safe passage out of Iroquoia without the risk of possession by the Otkon. In effect, severing the head and placing it upon a pole was seen by the Indians as sacrificing the soul of the victim to the evil spirit in return for immunity.

A necessary part of the sacrifice, in both cases, involved the ritual of placing the severed head on a pole that had special meaning in the Indian spirit world. One, the skull on a post indicated that the soul of the victim had been sacrificed to the evil spirit. Two, the skull served as both a visual and spirit-world image that the person who had severed the head of the victim was protected from possession by the evil spirit, thus affording himself immunity. Three, the skull on a post let all Indians know that the place where it stood was unequivocally a place of evil. So if it served as a warning to others, **the warning was for all Indians**, and not white men, who did not believe in the ideas of the Indian spirit world. Consequently, all Indians who heard the story of what transpired at Wheeling Creek, but had never visited the place and knew it only by its name, understood one thing clearly. Weel-lunk, Place of the Skull, was a cursed place for Indians. Place of the Skull was an evil place, inhabited by an evil spirit that possessed white men to do evil things to Indians.

Place of the Skull

Part Four:
A Legacy of Evil

Place of the Skull

Chapter 10: The Place of Evil Touches Logan

The Cayuga Iroquois warrior named Taghneghdorus, the Spreading Oak, [117] slowly crumbled to his knees and buried his head in his hands, in shocking disbelief. Before him lay a gruesome scene of mutilated Indian bodies lying in the center of his village on Yellow Creek. Taghneghdorus, who had been called back to the village with his hunting party from deep in the interior of the Ohio Country, had only been told that something terrible had happened. He had not expected to find the bodies of thirteen of his family and friends who had been slain. Looking upon their faces wrapped in death, Taghneghdorus began to weep, as he had not done since the death of his mother twenty-seven years ago. The remaining members of the small Mingo village stood together in stark silence watching the man they considered their chief and war captain slowing rock back and forth in grief. Finally, a high pitched mourning wail came from his mouth, and grew louder and louder, signaling each Indian to join in the death song and express the pain that all felt for the loss of so many people in the close-knit village who were dear to all of them. At the center of them, Taghneghdorus, the man that Indians and whites alike had come to call by the English name Logan, was inconsolable.

Logan had been away hunting buffalo up the trail leading away from his village on Yellow Creek when his family was lured across the Ohio River by a party of white men bent on murdering Indians. Logan, always a friend to whites, was in disbelief that it had happened. Since the time he was a boy with his mother and father at their village in Pennsylvania, Logan had

163

been taught by his father, the Oneida Iroquois chief Shickellamy, [118] to be a friend of the English at all times. Shickellamy had been instrumental over the years in guiding Iroquois and Delaware relations with the English. He had forged a chain of friendship and peace with the whites through his efforts, and that of Pennsylvania's ambassador to the Iroquois, Conrad Weiser, who Shickellamy was fond of. Those had been years of relative peace, Logan often remembered, where he could roam the Susquehanna Valley lands without fear of white men. But that peace had come to an end all too soon. In the year 1747, Logan's mother, a Cayuga Iroquois from whom he inherited his blood line, had died from a white man's epidemic. The next year, his father Shickellamy died too, of a broken heart, some said, and left John Shickellamy, as his father called him, and two brothers and two sisters to make their own way in a changing Indian world where the white man was increasingly taking away Indian land from underneath their feet.

When the French stirred the Iroquois, Shawnee, and Delaware in 1755 to join them in a war against the English frontier to end their land grab of Indian lands once and for all, John Shickellamy, now calling himself Logan, led councils with the Pennsylvania Iroquois petitioning them to remain neutral in the coming war. This caused him to make many enemies of his Indian brothers who had taken up the hatchet against the despised English. Logan, remembering the words of his father, would not change his mind on the matter, and refused to accept the black wampum belt and the red hatchet. However, due to the enmity of the hostile Delaware towards Logan and a handful of neutral Iroquois, Conrad Weiser had thought it better than Logan and his family, and the others, be escorted away from their homes on the frontier to Weiser's in the event that hostile Delaware and Shawnee made good on their threat to "knock them on the heads," after giving the Shickellamys and Scarroyady much "ill language." [119] Logan sat out the war. He prided himself on the decision to do so, saying years later, "During the course of the last long and bloody war, Logan remained idle in his cabin, an advocate of peace. Such was my love for the whites." [120] Logan was all-the-more vindicated for his decision when the war turned in favor of the English. General Forbes with Washington pushed an army west over the mountains to destroy the French fort at the Forks of the Ohio, and soon the Delaware and Shawnee came back to the English with their tails between their legs, licking their wounded pride in having taken sides in the war at all.

Also, Logan had kept his peace, and his tongue, when some of his people visiting the village of Conestoga Town were murdered by a mob of Scotch-Irish whites from Paxtang bent on killing Indians in revenge for the war incited by the Ottawa chief Pontiac, and cared not who the peaceful Indians were. The Governor placed sixteen Conestoga Indians in a jailhouse in Lancaster for their own protection. Soon, twenty-five to thirty mounted white men calling themselves the Paxton Boys broke into the jail and killed every man, women and child inside with guns and tomahawks. William Henry of Lancaster was a witness to the horrid results, writing, "A man's hands and feet had been chopped off with a tomahawk. In this manner lay the whole of them, men, women and children, spread about the prison yard: shot-scalped-hacked-and cut to pieces." [121] The act was called murder by Pennsylvania authorities, but no white man was brought to justice for the killing of these peaceful Indians, Logan recalled. Still, Logan rejected the longing within him to seek justice on his own, by vengeance killing, saying later, "The white people killed my kin at Coneestoga a great while ago, and I thought nothing of that." [122] Nonetheless, Logan heeded the implicit message from the English settlers that all Indians were no longer welcome in eastern Pennsylvania. Quietly, Logan moved his family and those Cayuga friends who would follow him to the mouth of Yellow Creek on the Ohio River below Logstown in the Ohio Country where he made a new home for himself, and maintained his reputation of a friend to whites.

Now, all of this that Logan thought himself to be in the eyes of the whites had come to an abrupt end. Logan felt his world turned completely upside down as he writhed in inconsolable grief, looking upon the faces of those he held dear him, so terribly slain. Immediately before Logan lay his wife Mellana; horribly bludgeoned to death, and her scalp torn from her head. Next to her lay Logan's younger brother, Tahgajute known by the English as James, a grimace of pain still visible on his face. He had been shot twice, and his scalp taken. Beside Logan's brother lay his brother's son, Mohnah, also shot and scalped. However, these three corpses of his immediate family paled in comparison when Logan gazed upon that of his own sister, Koonay, called Anne by the English. Anne had been carrying her youngest child of Colonel John Gibson [123] in a papoose board strapped to her back, as she had been pregnant and ready to give birth to their newest child in several weeks. The little baby girl in the back board was gone, and by all appearances, Anne had been beaten so severely before she died that her face was unrecognizable. Worse of all, the men who had done this to her had opened her belly with a knife while she was still alive and disemboweled her and the fetus, taking both their scalps before stabbing them lifeless. The sight of Anne and her lifeless unborn child was more than Logan could bear and he let out a shriek that could be heard across the river at Baker's now abandoned cabin.

After a period of time passed, Logan pulled himself together and spoke in Iroquois to those men who had been able to retrieve the bodies. Logan wanted to know how this had happened and who had done it. From them, Logan learned that two Shemanese, the name given to those white men that called themselves Virginians, had come to the village three days ago. No one had seen them before, however they acted friendly. The two Shemanese invited anyone who wanted, to cross the river to John Baker's trading cabin, to gamble, shoot at marks, and drink rum the next day. Logan's brother and his son agreed to do so; at the last minute Logan's wife and sister decided to go along to look over the goods at Baker's. It was not long before those in the village heard gunshots and women's screams, and decided at once to paddle across to see what had happened. Close to shore they were ambushed by white men hidden behind trees along the shoreline. Caught by surprise, they made easy targets due to their helplessness in the canoes. As a result, several men were killed or wounded before they could turn around and paddle out of gunshot range. There was nothing more they could do. The whites outnumbered them and prevented anyone from coming close enough to get off a shot of their own. Those killed in the canoes were brought here first, and when the Shemanese left, the remaining men from the village were able to retrieve Logan's family members and friends, all thirteen in number. [124]

The look of studied enquiry on Logan's face gradually changed into one of growing anger as he listened intently to what had been told to him. Whites had done this to his family and friends. Whites, that

167

Logan professed friendship for, whites that Logan had always fed if they came to his cabin hungry, and gave clothes to them if they were, as he described, as "cold and naked." It was not the whites of Pennsylvania that had destroyed the only family he had, and wiped his seed from the earth. It was the Shemanese, the Virginians that the Shawnee called the "Long Knifes" who for no reason, not one of vengeance or retaliation, had killed Logan's family. Logan could not understand why. There was no reason for any white man to do what had been done. However, that changed when Logan asked if anyone knew where these men had come from and where they had since gone. It was unanimous among the Mingos reporting, that the Shemanese had come from and returned to the same place—Kanororan, the place of evil.

Kanororan downriver was that place of evil where the mouth of the creek flowed into the O-yee-O, with the island. Logan knew the word Kanororan and understood its meaning as Place of the Skull, the place of evil white men's magic, and the place of the evil spirit, Otkon. Now Logan knew beyond a doubt what had happened. That evil spirit and evil place where it dwelled would not rest until all Indians were destroyed and the land within its reach cleared. It had a new ally to do its bidding—the Shemanese who had proved without a doubt that they were evil, sent to chastise Logan for his friendship to whites. The evil spirit in the Shemanese had come seeking Logan himself but Logan had been protected by his own magic. Unfortunately, his family and his friends did not have that protection, and the Otkon would not rest unless Indian blood was spilled, Indian scalps were taken, and Indian souls were devoured. The Otkan was a white evil spirit that Logan was sure of. The story told around the campfires said that Place of the Skull was a white man's skull put on

168

the post to protect that Indian who had sought vengeance and appeased the spirit with the white man's soul. But now the Otkon had been roused again and had come for Logan, and even now taunted him with the sight of the bodies of his wife, sister, and brother.

Logan plotted his revenge long and hard. It was not a question of not doing so, in his mind. It was a matter of fulfilling vengeance without falling into the grasp of the Otkan. Did the evil spirit in the Shemanese have a name, Logan asked the warriors? Yes, he was told, the name of the white man was Cresap, the Shemanese from the Potomac. A Delaware coming up river the day before the Shemanese arrived, had said that the whites at Weel-luk had gathered to hear a Shemanese named Cresap boast about starting an Indian war by killing all Indians he could find. "He would put every Indian he met with on the river to death, if he could raise men," the Delaware related. [125] Cresap and the men he found were to blame for cold-blooded, unprovoked murder of these innocent people of Logan's, "not sparing even my women and children." [126] With his mind now set with his plan for revenge, Logan made his vow to the warriors gathered around him. He would seek vengeance on the Shemanese only; not the Pennsylvanians. Logan would stay out of reach of the evil spirit at Kanororan; he would not attack the Virginians there directly. That, he believed, is what the white Otkan, and Cresap wanted him to do. No, he would not be so foolish to do so, but would take the lives of innocent Shemanese living away from Kanororan— all who might fall into his hands and under the blade of his hatchet and knife, until thirteen scalps, and more were taken. Many more would fall under his knife for the death of his sister and unborn child, and he would do so, not sparing man, woman, or child, just as none of his had been spared. Logan would see to it that the Otkan, and Cresap, felt Logan's fury, for he would take away from them what had been taken away from him. Then looking up skyward, and invoking the protection of the Great Spirit to give Logan the strength for as long as he should live, Logan cried out, "There now runs not a drop of my blood in the veins of any living creature. This calls on me for REVENGE!" [127]

By June 30 of that year, Logan and his war party had returned to Yellow Creek to gather up their things and remove themselves into the interior of the Ohio Country, far away from the Shemanese who were looking for him in particular as a large scale war between Indians and whites was eminent. Logan himself had thirteen scalps of the Shemanese to hang from his belt, to be stretched and dried on hoops to show that he had sought vengeance for those of his slain friends and family by taking the lives of those who were likewise innocent, in retaliation. It was recorded that "Logan says, he is now satisfied for the loss of his Relations, and will sit Still until he hears what the Long Knife…will say." [128]

Chapter 11: At the Gates of Evil

The Mingo, Delaware, and Shawnee had kept an eye on Weel-lunk now that whole scale war by the Shemanese was underway. The Place of the Skull had been a beehive of activity. A small fort had been erected there on the bluff above the mouth of the creek by the Virginian named McDonald with over a hundred men to cut down the trees, trim the poles, and erect them in the ground to form a crude palisade with a gate. The fort would be called Fincastle by the whites, and would serve as a staging area for frontier militia and their scouting parties. The white man named Zane, who had a brother living with the Wyandots in the Ohio Country since their capture as children, had a hand in building the fort. He and another man named Caldwell had supervised its construction, which was erected near Zane's own home. [129] The Indians could not understand this man Zane. He had willingly built his home under the shadow of the Place of the Skull, yet by all appearances, he had not taken part in the killing of Logan's family, nor did he show any sign of embracing the evil in the place where he now built his own fire. In the months after the deaths of Logan's family, Logan had been told that Zane had been heard by others trying to discourage Cresap and his men from doing harm to Logan, Zane himself saying, "This measure I opposed with much violence alleging that the killing of these Indians, Logan and his family, might bring about a war if they succeeded." [130] The Shemanese had paid no attention to Zane and war had come to the frontier. Now three years later, war was about to come again.

In the spring of the year 1777, the head man for the English King across the waters, a man named Hamilton, had issued a call for all the tribes of the Ohio

Country to come with their warriors and families to Detroit, to hear what the great King wanted him to tell them, about the war between the English Father and his disobedient child, the Yankees. By the scores, the Mingo, Delaware, Wyandot and Shawnee from the lands bordering the Ohio River and the white frontier settlements had come to council. Many others were there too, including the tribes of Lake Indians, and those from the western lands of the Illinois Country. A great many tents and temporary bark shelters had been erected for the councils to be held with Hamilton, who made sure that all the Indians in attendance were well fed, and given copious presents, especially for the women and children. A great many councils were held over the ensuing days, and much was talked about and smoked over, as each tribe debated the matters discussed. Hamilton had told them that the English King, their Father, had lost his patience with his unruly son, the Yankees, and the time had now come to punish the Yankees and put them in their place by not sparing them the rod. The English were sending a massive army across the great waters to Canada to invade the lands of the Bostonians by way of the Champlain Lake, and elsewhere. What their Father needed, more than anything else, was the support of his Indian children here in the Ohio Country, to drive the hated Shemanese back across the mountains and punish them for their abuse of the King's own red children.

Hamilton's speeches had struck a chord with the tribes. Each discussed in their own way among their head men the proposal of the English Hamilton, with War Captains and Village Captains alike having their own time to talk, and give their opinion. While they had managed to stay out of this war between the white Father and his unruly son up to this point, there was much resentment and ill-will towards the Shemanese along the Indian frontier, with hostile acts against Indians perpetrated by the Virginians every time they encountered an Indian on the trail or in the water. The Shemanese at their town called Pitt at the Forks of the Ohio had half-heartedly called the Indians to council with them, but the risk had been too great for many headmen to attend. It was well-known that the whites there had few presents and no powder or lead to give the Indians as a token of their good-will. Here, the English King would provide them with everything they would need, including provisions for their families while the warriors were away and red-coated soldiers with the fire sticks called cannon to drive the Shemanese out. As the council neared its close, the assembled Indians waited patiently to hear Hamilton speak one more time, to know what his words were.

Hamilton, resplendent in his red officer's coat, rose from his seat before the huge assembly of over fifteen hundred Indians, and began his argument to them in words that they could understand from the trusted translators. "Let us give thanks to the Master of Life, the Great Spirit to whom we all serve, for having preserved us and given us so clear a sky this day to hear the words of your Father, the King of England, who is sorrowful for the pain inflicted upon his children by the Rebels," began Hamilton. He then went on to ask the Indians what their Father needed of them, promising that if they picked up the "Red hatchet of war" against the Shemanese that their Father would reward them with all the lands that they rid of the white settlers, as once again their rightful possession, that had so grievously been stolen from them without asking. "Children! The King has ordered me to give you His War Axe that he wishes to be used to drive the Rebels from the rivers that water your hunting grounds." A murmur of agreement arose from the Indian assemblage when they heard Hamilton's words as there was not one Indian present who had not seen with their own eyes the truth of Hamilton's words.

Hamilton would see to it that the warriors would get new English muskets; and plenty of gun powder, lead ball, scalping knives, and shining new hatchets that had not as yet been washed in the blood of the Shemanese. Said Hamilton, "You must remember that when you receive your Father's War Axe, I tell you he will have attention to your necessities while you act the part of dutiful children. I tell you that what you will receive does not come from me but from the King, your Father, who has thought of you, though at so great a distance, and has sent you ammunition, clothing, and other matters necessary for you. Children! I tell you the truth. Your Father's design is to satisfy all his children." All that was needed was the agreement of the head men of the tribes that they would send their war parties to raid the frontier settlements along the east side of the Ohio, from the place called Fort Pitt down the river to the mouth of the Kanawha and further into Kan-tuck-Kee; wherever the hated Shemanese Virginians could be found. Closing the Grand Council after several days, Hamilton concluded by saying, "Having returned thanks to the Great Spirit, I must thank you all for having attended to my call, in coming to the Council fire, which I hope shall continue to burn clear and bright, which round we shall renew this union again and again, and brighten the chain of friendship between your Father the King, and his children, that shall last while the Sun and Moon give light to the World."

Hamilton had been successful. The war captains and head men agreed to his proposition to attack the frontier by summer, but each at places of their own choosing and their own time, of which Hamilton had no say. A handful of trusted French men at Detroit would accompany the war parties to the frontier, as they were able to speak the Indian dialects and could relay back to Hamilton any needs that the Indians may have. Beyond that, the English commander at Detroit was powerless to do more, and would have to take the Indians on their word that they would fulfill the wishes of their English Father across the water. When the headmen of the many clans of the tribes returned to their mixed villages in the Ohio Country, they met in council to discuss where and when their warriors would strike, and for how long. Some of the hot-blooded younger warriors set out immediately along the paths to the Ohio River, unable to wait any longer to attack the whites. Others waited, and counseled what the best place to strike might be.

By mid-summer, Shawnee and Wyandot war parties began returning from the Virginian frontier with plunder, horses, prisoners and scalps to their villages on the Scioto and Upper Sandusky. The Mingo and Delaware had sent some small war parties across the Ohio River to raid the outlying settler cabins wherever they could be found; however, there was much disagreement in the major village of Goschachgunk as to what was to be done. The Mingo wished to attack the Shemanese at Kanororan to settle scores and uproot the evil whites there. The Delaware war captains counseled that it was against the accepted, wise way for warriors to fight. To attack a white man's fort from which they could shoot down anyone approaching the walls was foolishness, as many men would be lost without being able to breach the walls, since they had no cannon. When asked about cannon, the Frenchman LaMotte, from Detroit, shook his head. There would be none forthcoming, as they could not be brought over the paths from Detroit. However, the Mingo insisted that they find some way to attack the evil whites, including Cresap and his men, whom they believed to be still there. Finally, a compromise was reached. A major attack was planned for the late summer, against the place the Mingos wished to destroy more than anywhere else. It was agreed that the combined warriors would mind the advice of the war captains and attempt to lure the Shemanese out of the fort by guile, and then ambush them. Once that was done, if possible, no attempt would be made against the fort itself. Kanororan, The Place of the Skull, and the place better known now as the town of the white man's evil towards Indians, would be attacked, and hopefully destroyed.

Stealthily, the war party of three hundred and fifty Mingo, Delaware, Shawnee, and Wyandot warriors crossed the Ohio River at the fording place several miles above Kanororan and made their way under the cover of darkness to the fields surrounding the fort. Scouts had arrived earlier in the day, and posted themselves undetected upon the hill overlooking the fort, now called Patrick Henry, watching the Shemanese inside coming and going. At dark, the scouts met the arriving Indians and discussed the best possible places for the warriors to hide themselves in the cornfields in preparation for a morning ambush. The scouts had counted heads. It appeared that there were some forty Shemanese militia inside the fort who had been seen drilling, in addition to the settlers who lived outside the walls, and the Zanes. Six Mingo warriors were chosen to open the ambush, which would involve them appearing on the path that led away to the southeast of the fort walls, where they would fire upon the fort, making the Shemanese believe that they were only a small war party bent of killing livestock. [131]

The ambush was sprung shortly after daybreak when a white man and his Negro were encountered on the path, looking for horses. The white man was shot and killed, but the Negro allowed to escape towards the fort, so as to mislead the Shemanese into thinking that there were only six warriors. The whites outside the fort hurriedly ran to the still open gate with their women and children. Very soon a soldier captain at the head of fourteen Shemanese militiamen came from the fort to attack the six warriors, whereupon several hundred Indians in hiding rose and fired their guns, killing or wounding all of the men. Hearing the firing from outside the fort, another company of militia attempted to come to the rescue of their comrades but was ambushed as well. Zane had counseled the second group to not leave the fort, as the Indians had set a trap, but his advice did not save them, and they too were killed, scalped and mutilated, along with the rest. With no one else willing to leave the protection of the fort, the warriors whooped with glee, and proceeded to kill all the livestock outside the fort walls, and burn the cabins and barns after loading themselves down with the plunder, which was placed upon the captured horses. Unfortunately, there were no prisoners to be taken across the river, and not nearly enough scalps for all the warriors present in the battle to satisfy them with. But with the element of surprise gone, so went the possibility of any future ambush. The fort could not be taken by any other means than a costly frontal attack that all warriors were abhorrent of attempting, knowing it would result in the needless loss of life. The Indian captains decided that it was time to withdraw across the river before the Shemanese sent a relief force that would not fall for an ambush as this foolish militia had done.

At the makeshift Indian camp that night, the captains discussed over pipes of tobacco what had transpired during the day. They agreed that they had been successful in the ambush, having killed many

Shemanese without losing warriors slain. Many scalps had been taken and now hung from the belts of the warriors who could show them as a sign of their bravery in battle. Too, horses had been taken, along with a great deal of plunder that would prove useful back in their home villages. In all, they agreed that a significant blow had been struck against the Shemanese at the fort at Weel-lunk but not the blow that they had all wished for. The fort at Place of the Skull still stood, through no fault of their own. The war captain Zane who lived there had survived, and would not come out from behind the walls to fight them. Perhaps, a Delaware captain queried, Zane had a knowing or seen a vision of the plan of their head men to launch a surprise attack by ambush and that is why he did not come out. A Mingo captain thought that perhaps the evil spirit residing at Kanororan had spoken to Zane alone, telling him not to go out, and advising him to convince the other whites not to do so too. Although the whites had lost much during the day's battle, they could still muster a great deal of magic from the place to avert their total destruction. That was the evil spirit's doing as far as the Indians were concerned. It would allow the deaths of some whites while preserving others, the ones that it wanted to keep, to use in the future for its ruin of the Indians. Zane had been spared. No one could kill him, nor could they kill the Shemanese McColloch who rode his horse over a cliff and survived, to escape the pursuing warriors. Yes, a blow had been struck at Weel-lunk but the evil there, in the form of the shrewd whites doing its bidding against Indians, had not been uprooted.

Chapter 12: The Nest of Snakes Grows

By 1781, the war for the Ohio Country between the Indians and the Virginians had entered its fifth year with no end in sight. Many of the Virginian Shemanese living along the east bank of the Ohio River and in the Ken-tuck-ee lands had been killed by the Indians and their homes, barns, and settlements burned to ashes, but more white men arrived from across the mountains in the east to take their place in spite of all the Indians and the British could do to stop them. There had been major successes by the Indians with their allied English brothers like the Girtys, McKee, and Elliott fighting alongside them. Together, they had been able to chase away the Shemanese back to Pitt from their fledgling fort they called Laurens on the Muskingum River. Too, the campaign into the Ken-tuck-ee lands to the south had brought about the destruction of several forts the previous year with the help of the red-coat Captain Bird and his men with their cannon. Many scalps, prisoners, horses, and plunder had been taken back to their villages. However, the Shemanese Long Knife Captain named Clark had surprised the Shawnee during the late summer by attacking their villages up the Big and Little Miami Rivers, and destroying the villages and the cornfields before the warriors who were away could come back to fight him. All of the women and children were able to escape to the woods, and only a few Shawnee defenders were killed and wounded during their fighting withdrawal to escape from the mounted Shemanese. Many Shemanese were believed to be struck down, but greater damage was done to the Shawnee. Their homes were pillaged and burnt; their horses taken, and their corn and squash for the winter completely lost. Yes, the Shawnee would survive to fight again, but like a tree whipped about by a thunderstorm, the Shawnee were severely shaken by Clark and his men who came out of nowhere, and without warning.

The English at Detroit sent McKee and Elliot with food and supplies to the Shawnee to bolster them and encourage the warriors to resume their raids in the spring, but the Shawnee were clearly demoralized for the moment. Together, they abandoned their former villages close to the Virginians and moved deeper into the Ohio Country, to put greater distance between them and Clark across the Ohio, and to make help from Detroit easier to come by. Nonetheless, the Shawnee were wary of a new attack from Clark, and told their white brothers with them that they wished to stay closer to their homes. They feared that the Shemanese would come again, and next time kill all their defenseless women and children while the warriors were away attacking the frontier elsewhere. Their fears were not unfounded; however it was the Delaware who were struck next. This time the Shemanese came from Weel-lunk, the Indians believed, intending to kill all the Delaware men, women, and children they could find. In the late spring, a militia army under the command of a General named Brodhead had come down the Ohio River from Pitt with his soldiers and put their boats in at the fort at Weel-lunk to ask the militiamen there to join them. Crossing the Ohio, a force of almost three hundred Shemanese surprised the Delaware village of Goschachgunk (Coshocton) on the Muskingum River. Brodhead's men who were on horses quickly surrounded the village, allowing only a few warriors to escape. In the village they found thirty-five old men and boys, and a few warriors. Also, four women and a handful of children were captured, and the men from Weel-lunk told their General that they wished to kill all the Indians.

180

The warriors who escaped the militiamen watched from a distance across the river. The General wanted to take all the Indian prisoners with him back to Pitt, but the Shemanese from Weel-lunk argued against that, saying that all the Delaware captives should be slain on the spot. Brodhead tried to stop them but he could not, and so he asked the Weel-lunk whites to at least spare the women, children, and elderly men. When this was finally agreed upon, fifteen Delaware men were condemned to death because the Delaware Indian named Pekillion who was advising the Shemanese general said that these men that he pointed out were warriors. The fifteen Delaware had their hands bound and were separated from the others. Once done, the evil white men from Weel-lunk took them and one-by-one and killed them by sinking tomahawks in their heads before scalping them, and then mutilating their bodies beyond recognition. The village was pillaged of all Indian goods, and then the homes were burnt. Satisfied that they had sated themselves with the blood of the Delawares, the militiamen voted to return to Weel-lunk against Brodhead's wishes who wanted to continue up the river further. The furs and livestock plunder was taken to Weel-lunk where it was sold to the local residents and fetched a handsome price.

While they were preparing to leave, a Delaware headman some believed was Coquetageghton, known by the English as White Eyes, or Red Hawk, called from across the river, asking Brodhead to council with him. It was said that the Delaware headman had been a friend to the Virginians, like those Delaware who lived with the white Christian preachers several miles away. Montour the half-breed Shemanese scout with Brodhead told him that the chief wanted to talk peace for the Delaware who were not hostile to the Virginians, and would cross the river to do so if Brodhead would promise he would not be killed. Brodhead agreed and motioned for the Indian to come across. After beaching his canoe and approaching the Shemanese General to counsel, a white man from Weel-lunk appeared from the bushes and approaching the Delaware chief from behind, pulled a tomahawk out of his blouse and struck the Indian in the back of his head with it, killing the Delaware chief instantly, much to the delight of the others from Weel-lunk who cheered him. The white devil was known to be one of the brothers named Wetzel who lived at Weel-lunk and spent their time on the paths on the west side of the Ohio looking for Indians to ambush. On the march to Weel-lunk with the Delaware captives, it was believed that Wetzel killed many more, if not all, not sparing women or children to satisfy his thirst for Indian blood and their scalps. This white man Wetzel [132] was, without a doubt, the hand of Weel-lunk evil that was looking for Indian souls to devour, and extending its arms everywhere like snakes leaving a nest.

The Shemanese named Clark was known to be at Weel-lunk as well, planning to raise an army to attack not only the Shawnee again but Detroit itself and destroy all the Indians allied with the British. Clark brought many new Virginians to Weel-lunk which had grown in size, said Indian scouts hidden in the trees across the Ohio River. Boats were observed coming and going from Pitt with men, horses, and supplies unloaded at Weel-lunk. Soldiers drilled on the open ground around the fort, and occasionally men shot their rifles in target practice to prepare for future attacks on the Indians, that were sure to come against the Shawnee and Delaware before the year was out. Word spread throughout the Indian villages of the Ohio Country hostile to the Shemanese, that Weel-lunk was the center of all activity by Clark and his army that was designing to attack them.

It was apparent to Indians who heard this story that the white man's evil against all Indians had substantially grown since the first attack against the fort in 1777. Now no Indian would be able to attack Weel-lunk and destroy it. Its power was too great, and the evil had many heads that no one tribe could possibly kill, like Clark, Wetzel, Brodhead, Cresap, Zane and others. Blood lust was on the minds of the whites, and so it was important that the Indians remain vigilant that they were not surprised again by the Shemanese.

That vigilance on the part of the Delaware scouts watching Weel-lunk paid off. They relayed the message by runners that Clark and his army of four hundred men left Weel-lunk by boat on the morning of August 7th, headed down the Ohio River for what must likely be a planned strike against the Shawnee and Detroit. [133] No doubt Clark was on his way to the small fort he had erected at the Falls of the Ohio, which he would use for a jumping off point into the Ohio Country. As the runners were set in motion to warn the Shawnee, a second force of Virginians arrived at Weel-lunk by boat from Pitt the next day with one hundred men and horses in horse-boats. New runners were sent in haste down the paths once it was seen that this force left soon after to rendezvous with Clark. Indian eyes followed the boats from the shoreline and finally an opportunity presented itself to ambush the Shemanese boats near Big Bone Lick on the Ohio. The Mohawk Thayendanega, known as Brant, and the combined warriors with him and one of the Girtys were far downriver when Clark's boats approached during the night. In the dark, the warriors were unable to ambush Clark as he and his men passed by them. However, word reached them in time to set up an ambush for the second boat flotilla following Clark by a day. All of the one hundred Shemanese were killed or captured, and many scalps and plunder were taken. Some of the power of the Shemanese from Weel-lunk had been sapped, which was promising to the Delaware, Shawnee and Mingo in particular. The Girty brother told them that Clark would be unable to attack the Shawnee and Detroit without the men and supplies which were lost, which proved to be correct.

In the late summer, it was decided in council at Detroit that Elliot and the Wyandot Half King, with the consent of the Delaware headmen Hopocan, named Captain Pipe, that the Christian Delawares living with the white preachers on the upper Muskingum Rivers should be removed to the Upper Sandusky villages. It was known that Heckewelder and Zeisberger were asking their Indian converts to inform on the comings and goings of the Delaware war parties crossing the Ohio River from the Ohio Country to raid the white settlements. Now had come the time to cut off the ears and blind the eyes of the Weel-lunk evil so that it could not kill more Delaware as had been done in the past by the preachers relaying word on the Delaware to Zane at the fort there. One of the weaknesses of the white man's evil was that it did not have eyes and ears of its own. It could not see and hear deep into the forests and observe the Indians in their villages it wished to destroy.

The Indians and their white brothers still had advantage in this one area, and if the white preachers were taken away once and for all from the grasp of Weel-lunk, it would be more helpless than before, in that regard. Consequently, in August, Elliot and the Delaware and Wyandot warriors were able to capture the preachers and their converts without violence. Elliot spoke to the Christian Indians, explaining to them why it was necessary for them to abandon their villages. "I see you live in a dangerous place. Two powerful and mighty spirits or gods are standing and opening wide their jaws

184

toward each other to swallow both. And between them, you are placed. You are in danger, from one or from the other, or even from both. Therefore I take you by the hand, raise you up, and settle you where I dwell." [134] What Elliot was telling them was that the Great Spirit of the Indians and the Evil Spirit of the whites at Weel-lunk were at war; the outcome yet undecided. Of the ominous signs Zeisberger was feeling, he wrote at the time, "We felt the power of darkness, as if the air was filled with evil spirits." [135]

And so it was done. The Christian Delaware were removed and the white preachers made prisoners of the Wyandot Half King. While the several hundred Indians headed northwest along the paths to the Upper Sandusky villages with what possessions they could carry, a large war party of Delaware, Mingo, and Wyandot warriors separated themselves from the main body. It was decided by the War Captains to follow the paths that led to Weel-lunk, and strike a blow against the Shemanese now that Clark and his soldiers were gone down river. Too, now there were no informers who could give the Shemanese warning of their approach. The war party wished to ambush the fort defenders as had been done the previous time, but that was not about to be. Zane who was present in the fort was now the eyes and ears of Weel-lunk, and as so, he was ever vigilant and shrewdly informed to his ears only of any hostile Indians within his immediate area. No whites would come out to engage the handful of Indians who exposed themselves to the fort while the rest waited in hiding in the surrounding fields. It was apparent to the Indians that the evil spirit residing in its nest at Weel-lunk knew the Indian design and informed Zane, who thought it prudent to keep all whites within the strengthened fort. Finally, the war party decided to withdraw but not before once again burning the settler cabins and killing all the livestock so as to starve those in the fort.

No Shemanese blood had been spilled, and no scalps taken by the warriors, yet they were exultant with the plunder and horses that they had been able to take with them back to the Upper Sandusky. All in all, the venture had some modest success. It appeared to the Indians that they had driven back the Shemanese at Weel-lunk for the moment, as they were unwilling to come out of the fort. For the Delaware, vengeance for the deaths of their relatives at the village of Goschachgunk had not been fulfilled at yet. Perhaps, some said, the white evil spirit at Weel-lunk had been subdued by the deaths of the Shemanese down the river who had resided at Weel-lunk, and by the removal of the Christian Delaware and their white spies. Perhaps the Great Spirit had shown the evil at the Place of the Skull that the Indians were mighty and would prevail and put it to sleep once and for all, and drive all the whites away, including Zane.

How wrong the Indians were. They did not anticipate the move of the evil of Weel-lunk to retaliate against the Indians. They did not comprehend the reach of its arm and its ability to strike them so quickly and so deeply. It was not subdued; it was not asleep at all. It was as if it had taunted the Indians with modest successes to lull them into a prideful state. And that pride was blind to the disaster that was about to befall them.

Chapter 13: Massacre and Murder comes from Weel-lunk

What the Delaware did not realize was they had let their guard down after their attack on the fort at Weel-lunk, and their withdrawal to the Upper Sandusky villages in preparation for winter. No more war parties took to the paths leading to the frontier. This presented the Virginians with an opportunity in October to act. A shrewd Shemanese captain decided to take a small army of mounted militiamen drawn from Weel-lunk and the surrounding countryside into the Ohio Country to look for Indians to kill; specifically the Christian Moravian Delaware. Williamson was the name of this captain. He had had enough of the constant Indian raiding parties ravaging the Pennsylvania frontier that year, and so decided to take matters into his own hands when the other Virginians would not. Williamson enlisted nearly one hundred mounted men, including many who came from Weel-lunk. They crossed the Ohio River above Weel-lunk and made their way along the Indian path to the Moravian Delaware villages, but to their disappointment, found them all but deserted, save a few starving Christian Indians attempting to harvest corn that they had hastily left. [136] Williamson did not know that Elliott and the Half King had taken the Delaware and their Christian preachers away to the Upper Sandusky villages. Williamson wanted revenge on the Moravian Indians whom he suspected were giving food and shelter to the war parties attacking the frontier, and if he and his men could, they would put an end to those Indians once and for all. Angry at not finding the Moravian Delaware, the militiamen were forced to turn around and return home empty-handed without killing the "red vipers," as Williamson was known to call all Indians. However, he was not about to abandon his plan anytime soon.

The spring of 1782 was unusually mild, so the combined Mingo, Shawnee, Delaware, and Wyandot war parties commenced raiding across the Ohio River as soon as the snows thawed. The Indians chose to attack settlers in their isolated cabins and carry away captives and plunder. Just the fear alone of Indian raiding parties might be enough to drive the Shemanese out of their lands and back across the mountains, the Indians thought. Consequently, in early March, Williamson once again assembled his small army of militiamen to strike the Indians. Williamson's force crossed the Ohio River at Mingo Bottoms and followed the trail west towards the Moravian villages where he believed the Indian war parties were originating from. This, the Indians at the upper Sandusky villages did not know of. Coincidentally, nearly one hundred Christian Delaware had left those villages a week previously, and made their way to the deserted former homes. They were near starvation, and hoped to find whatever corn was not harvested from the previous autumn. Williamson's men surrounded the unarmed Delaware while they were working the fields, and took them to the village of Gnadenhutten to decide what was to be done with them.

The Christian Delaware professed their non-violent Christian neutrality to their captors, telling Williamson and his men that they had nothing to do with the hostile Indians who were raiding the frontier. Unfortunately, the militiamen found articles of clothing in one of the cabins which they believed belonged to a settler's wife who had been killed during a recent raid. The Indians explained that a Delaware had passed by only a day or two ago with the clothing and traded corn with them for the articles; however Williamson and his men would no longer hear any more pleas of their innocence. They convinced themselves that the Christian Indian men were guilty of taking part in the war parties, and the women and children of supporting them. In actuality, most of the militiamen cared little of whether the Indians were innocent or not. They wanted to kill all ninety-six of them all to be rid of the Indians once and for all, and Williamson agreed, though it mattered not that thirty-four of the Delaware were children as young as babies in their mothers' arms. Sixteen of the militiamen refused to take part in the morning execution which they considered outright murder. The Indians spent the night "in praying, singing hymns, and exhorting one another to die with the fortitude of Christians." [137]

The next morning Williamson's men went to work killing all the Moravian Indians, of whom more than two thirds were women and children. The victims were forced to kneel whereupon the white men, in an effort to save ammunition, used a cooper's mallet found in one of the cabins to hit the Indians on the head, crushing their skulls, before scalping each of them, including the youngest of children. "They were cruelly and shockingly murdered; and the different apartments of those houses of blood, exhibited their bleeding bodies, mangled by the tomahawk, scalping knife and spear, and disfigured by the war-club and the mallet. Thus perished ninety-six of the Moravians." [138] However, two Indian youths managed to escape; one who had been knocked down and scalped, but wasn't killed by the blow, and another who was able to slip through a trapdoor in the floor into the cellar below, and then out a window unobserved. Both made their way in haste to the Upper Sandusky villages to tell the hostile Delaware what had just happened. They related how their brethren had been brutally killed. Babies had their skulls crushed, and even newborns were ruthlessly scalped by the Shemanese. Then all of their bodies were burned in the buildings they had been killed in, some of whom were still alive. When this was done, the Shemanese left for Weel-lunk, laughing and boasting to each other the number of scalps they had taken. It was a story of absolute horror to all the Upper Sandusky Indians. The evil of the whites of Weel-lunk had intimately touched them.

The mourning for those family members who were slain went on for days. It was a dark sad time for the Indians. After grieving for this great loss, the Delaware as a people became enraged. The warriors vowed total bloody vengeance against any white man, woman, or child that should fall into their clutches in the future. Simon Girty, who was living with the Wyandots, was the first to let the British at Detroit know of the massacre of the Delaware innocents. In a letter he dictated to be sent to Major DePeyster, Girty reported, "The Moravians that went from Upper Sandusky this spring to fetch their Corn from their Towns where they lived last Summer, are all killed by the Virginian militia—the number of dead amounts to ninety-six Men, Women, and Children." [139] The Delaware counseled with the Mingo, Wyandot, and Shawnee as to where they might strike the Shawanese in retaliation. All were unanimous in wanting to attack Weel-lunk but a message was received from Alexander McKee that changed their plans. McKee, of the British Indian Department who was living with the Shawnee reported, "Two of the Scouting parties fell in with the Enemy on this side of the Ohio opposite to Weeling, on the road to Sandusky." The scouts had observed that the Shemanese were gathering an army of men "from the neighborhood of Weeling, designed against the Villages of Sandusky." [140] The Delaware realized that instead of going to war against the enemy, the hated evil Shemanese under Williamson were coming to them.

Hatchets and knives were sharpened, and guns repaired and made ready for the coming battle. Reinforcements in the form of green-coated British Rangers were called from Detroit. Ammunition and foodstuffs was distributed, and a call went out to all the warriors in the villages across the Ohio Country to join the Delaware in avenging the cruel deaths of their women and children. In addition, Indian scouts watched every move of the Shemanese army, counting heads at their rendezvous place at Mingo Bottom, and informing the Delaware and their allies at Upper Sandusky that the Shemanese army was almost five hundred mounted men. It was said that the Shemanese Colonel Crawford, a friend of many of the Delaware before the war, had joined Williamson in the campaign to wipe out the Upper Sandusky Indian villages and do to the women and children what had been done to the Moravians. The Delaware were not about to let that happen, and were eager to meet the Shemanese, as vengeance burned in their hearts as never before. They would not have long to wait.

In early June, the Shemanese army approached the first of the Indian villages that had been abandoned, and found no Indians. They stopped and were observed by Indian scouts to council with each other as to what was best to do. During the pause, the Rangers arrived from Detroit, along with Elliott with a reinforcement of warriors. McKee was soon to join the Delaware with the Shawnee. The decision was made to attack the Shemanese, who responded by forting up in a copse of woods, whereupon their entire army of whites was surrounded, and fired upon, causing many casualties. With no source of water in the woods, Williamson and Crawford decided that they should break out during the night and attempt to escape homeward by an orderly retreat. The Shemanese retreat turned into a rout, with many men killed and wounded. Fourteen were captured including Crawford and several of his officers the next day. Williamson, the source of evil at Gnadenhutten was one of those who escaped. In all, over half the Shemanese had been killed or wounded. The day after the rout, the Indians scoured the surrounding countryside, gathering horses, plunder, prisoners, and scalps of the dead Shemanese. It had been a joyous victory for all of the Indians and for the Delaware in particular. They had sought revenge for their own dead relatives, and fulfilled it against those who had committed the atrocity. Now there was one last act of vengeance to be dealt with—that of the Shemanese prisoners.

All of the militiamen were condemned to death. Many died on the spot as warriors who had relatives killed among the Moravians exacted their own personal revenge with tomahawk. Several were spared that fate so that they could be taken back to the Delaware women for to torture and burn in retribution. All remaining prisoners, save Crawford and his doctor were killed, scalped, mutilated, dismembered and fed to the village dogs. Crawford was stripped, beaten, and painted black signifying that he was condemned to be burned alive. Prior to his burning, Crawford pleaded for his life with the Delaware Captain Pipe, Wingemund, and Simon Girty, as each man knew Crawford prior to the war at Pitt, and were on the friendliest of terms. Girty attempted to buy Crawford from the Delaware to save his life, but was warned by them to cease or he would risk his own; Crawford must pay for the deaths of the Moravian Delawares, even though he had not been there himself.

In a last attempt, Crawford appealed to Wingemund, telling him that Williamson was the wicked man, not him. Wingemund agreed, but countered by asking Crawford what he was doing here at the Indian villages with the Shemanese, if he too did not have the intent of destroying the Indians? Nothing could save Crawford. Caldwell of the Rangers, who was wounded and taken to the lower Sandusky village, wrote to Detroit, "Simon Girty arrived last night from the Upper Village who informed me that the Delawares had burnt Colonel Crawford and two Captains at Pipe's Town, after torturing them a long time. Crawford died like a hero, never changed his countenance though they scalped him alive and then laid hot ashes upon his head after which they roasted him by a slow fire." [141] In Caldwell's mind, Crawford and his thirteen captured men got what they deserved at the hands of the Indians, summing it up by saying, "They came out on a party of pleasure," intending to kill more innocent women and children. [142] Vengeance had been fulfilled against the Shemanese. However, the source of white man's evil against Indians at Weel-lunk had not been destroyed, and again, one of the hands of that evil, Williamson, had managed to escape the grasp of the Indians due to what they believed was the evil spirit's protection from Weel-lunk. It was agreed in the councils held amongst the various tribes after the resounding defeat of the Shemanese at the Upper Sandusky that another attempt must be made to destroy Weel-lunk so as to free all Indians from its evil spell cast towards them.

Place of the Skull

Chapter 14: To Attack the Evil at Weel-lunk

After their great victory over the Shemanese at the Battle of the Upper Sandusky, the Indians wished to hold a council with their white allies, once Captain Caldwell of the Rangers was healed enough to attend. Caldwell had been shot through both buttocks early in the battle; one of the two Rangers who were wounded besides the one killed. Said Caldwell in a letter to Detroit, "I received a Ball through both my legs which obliged me to leave the field. If I had not been so unlucky, I am induced to think from the influence I have with the Indians, the Enemy would not have left the place we surrounded them in." [143] The Indians, on the other hand, had four killed and eight wounded, while they estimated more than one hundred militia had been killed, more than fifty wounded, and fourteen captured, including Crawford. To the Indians, the lopsided casualties were a result of the Great Spirit favoring them in battle; however the wounding of Caldwell was puzzling. Some went as far as to say that Caldwell's untimely misfortune had been caused by the evil Weel-lunk spirit attempting to exert its influence on the battle by thwarting the hand of the Great Spirit's white captain.

By late June, Caldwell called together all the headmen and war captains of the tribes in the Ohio Country to the Upper Sandusky villages to decide what would be the best course of action. The signs were favorable for further action against the enemy. Ammunition, food, and supplies had arrived from Detroit, along with another Ranger company soon to come from Niagara. However, the Indians were divided amongst themselves as to where to attack the Shemanese. Clark was known to be assembling men

195

from Kan-tuck-ee at the Falls of the Ohio for another planned attack on the Shawnee villages up the Big Miami River. Naturally, the Shawnee counseled that an attack should be made against Clark first, so as to eliminate the threat to their women and children once and for all. The Shawnee war captain, Snake rose and spoke directly to Caldwell. "Father! What we told you this Spring, it is needless to repeat, you granted it to us, your assistance came in good time. We have, with your People, defeated the Enemy. There is another army coming against us from Kenduck; that we are certain of, not only from prisoners, but from our young men who are watching them." [144] Snake paused to allow the interpreter James Girty to catch up with him, and then continued his speech to Caldwell.

"Father! We hope, if possible, You will send some more of your people and stores, such as is necessary for Warriors, with Cannon and Provisions sufficient to maintain the Indians. This you cannot do too soon." [145] Caldwell swallowed hard at Snake's mention of cannon, knowing that he would have the disagreeable responsibility to address the lack of forthcoming cannon at this very council before it was over. For the moment, Caldwell, McKee, Elliott, and the Girtys listened intently in silence as the Shawnee war captain Snake made the his argument to the rest of the assembled Indians. It was a convincing argument that made sense only to the Shawnee; however the Delaware were not in approval of it. When Snake was finished, the Wyandot Half King rose to speak to the council next. He reminded the Shawnee that while Clark had attacked their villages over a year ago, he had not been able to kill women and children as the Delaware had suffered at the Moravian villages. The Wyandot would not support a Shawnee attack against Clark until Delaware vengeance had been fully satisfied for their women and children so

196

horribly slain by the Shemanese evil to the east. The Wyandot would support the Delaware wishes, the Half King stated. It did not take long for the Mingo to agree also.

Captain Pipe and Wingemund rose to the assembled council and revealed their mind. Yes, Crawford and his captured men had paid dearly for their attempt to kill more women and children of the Delaware. The flesh of their own innocent people had been paid for with white flesh, but not nearly enough to satisfy anyone. This was because a heart of evil existed to the east at Weel-lunk which was intent on nothing less than the destruction of all Indians, not just the Delaware. The Delaware had been the first to feel the grievous injury that Weel-lunk was capable of inflicting. Something had to be done to eliminate the constant threat emanating from the source of white man's evil against all Indians. It could only be accomplished if all the Indians and their white allies under Caldwell fought as one body and attacked the Shemanese fort at Weel-lunk as soon as possible. Pipe advised that they should strike while the warriors were still free to do so, as it was not as yet the season for the men to go hunting and help in the harvest of the crops.

Captain Caldwell of the Rangers was not so sure. He had lived, worked, and fought alongside Indians since 1777, and knew their nature very well, and they ways of fighting. He understood how important fulfilling vengeance was to them, especially in this case, to the Delaware. Caldwell knew that seeking vengeance could drive the Indian warriors to do great things in battle they might normally not do, but he also knew that it could cloud their judgment too. In this case, Caldwell thought that may be happening. McKee, Elliott and the Girtys who lived closer to the Indians than he did, tried to

197

explain to him how the Indians believed that Weeling was the place of white man's evil for them. Caldwell tried to understand the Indian view that the place he called Weeling held an evil spirit that could only be eradicated if the settlement at Weeling, and the fort there, were destroyed. Caldwell did not know much about these things that the Indians alluded to—their world of manifest good and evil spirits. If he summed up what they were saying, he realized that a campaign against the fort at Weeling was deeply personal to them. The problem for Caldwell was that he was a white man; a military man ordered to conduct a military campaign against the Virginian frontier. Spirits or no spirits, attacking Weeling did not make a whole lot of sense to him.

When it was Caldwell's turn to speak to the assembled chiefs, he began by asking for those Indians who had been to Weel-lunk and seen the fort there to first tell him more about it, as he knew nothing of it. Caldwell was surprised at the response. Although every Indian seated before him intimately knew the story of the Place of the Skull and the evil towards Indians residing there, only two Indians had actually seen the fort from a vantage point across the Ohio River. Their descriptions were not a lot to go on, especially coming from Indians, but Caldwell was able to add to their information from that of the Girtys and Elliott. As best as Caldwell could guess, the frontier fort was about 120 feet square, sitting on a piece of high ground many hundred yards north from the creek mouth, with its west wall against the bluff facing the river. North of the picketed wall was a small ravine. To the east and south of the fort, the ground had been cleared some distance to give militia riflemen shooting from the parapets a clear field of fire against anyone approaching. To make matters worse, Caldwell learned that Zane had built his blockhouse several hundred feet to the south and east of that corner of the fort giving any shooters in Zane's blockhouse the ability to cover the approaches to the fort in many directions. In all, Caldwell thought that the fort and Zane's blockhouse had been well-placed with thought given to defending against an Indian attack.

What Caldwell had next to say to the Indians was going to be difficult, so he chose his words carefully. He knew that he needed to get the bad news on his mind out first before going further, or putting it off. The Indians would not be beyond blaming him if things did not go well, and they found out that he had kept something from them. Caldwell now told the Indians the truth they would not like to hear. He had received a dispatch some days ago from Major DePeyster in command of Fort Detroit, that no cannon would be forthcoming. DePeyster regretted the decision, but could not spare the men and material in light of the constant reports he was receiving that Clark was making ready to attack Detroit from his fort at the Falls of the Ohio, and an enemy army was mustering at Fort Pitt for a similar campaign. It was just that simple; the cannon could not be spared. The Indians, and Caldwell, would have to go it alone and make do with what they had at their disposal in any campaign against the frontier, Caldwell told the Indians. The news was met with a roar of disapproval and shouts from the Indians. Caldwell had no choice but to wait patiently until the Indians reaction subsided, so that he could speak again.

Reminding the Indians of his personal loyalty to them and his wish to strike the Shemanese together as brothers in this war, Caldwell asked the Delaware how they intended to attack the fort of Weeling. Captain Pipe responded, saying that he had given it much thought, knowing that the Indians were likely not to have British cannon to smash down the gates of the fort, and so must make do with another plan. First, he reminded everyone that the stratagem of an ambush had worked successfully in the attack on the fort in 1777, luring two companies of Shemanese militiamen out of the fort and into the ambush of the warriors. True, they had not been able to penetrate the fort, but the warriors had reduced the defenders greatly by the ambush which could work again, under the strictest of discipline on their parts to conceal their movements and presence. Secondly, if a ruse would not work, Caldwell could call on the fort defenders to surrender, granting them protection under the British flag, so as to entice them to open the gates, allowing the warriors to enter. And if both these plans should fail, Pipe believed that they could use the cover of the ravine to the north to bring combustibles to pile against the fort pickets while many Indian and Ranger guns kept up a steady fire against any defenders on the north wall attempting to stop them. The assemblage of Indians voiced their approval to Pipe's response.

Caldwell had serious doubts about Pipe's plans, and was sure that the War Captain's judgment was clouded, though he dared not insult Pipe in front of the other chiefs by confronting him outright. Caldwell was a veteran of many campaigns against Rebel militia forts. While the Rebel militia might be fools when attempting to fight Indians out in the open, they were not so foolish when fighting from inside a frontier fort where they had the decided advantage. Caldwell addressed Pipe directly, saying that he thought it highly unlikely that fort defenders could be lured into an ambush outside their fort a second time. Caldwell understood the fact that an ambush had been attempted unsuccessfully last fall, and that this Captain Zane at Weeling was too wise and experienced to let anyone out of the fort if he received an alarm, or spied a small party of Indians outside the walls.

The odds of an ambush working again were slim to none, in Caldwell's mind. Zane likely had scouts out on the paths across the river looking for Indian war parties so as to warn the fort. If the Indians were not seen during their approach, with the logistics of attempting to hide such a large force right under the nose of the Rebels, the chances of pulling it off were daunting. There was the high chance that a hot-headed young warrior would give them away during the time it would take to wait for the right opportunity for the defenders to come out of the fort and into the ambush, which might, in fact, never happen.

As to calling on the fort defenders to surrender under the protection of the King, Caldwell told Pipe and the chiefs to forget that notion. Every Virginian they had captured and interviewed since 1780 knew what had happened during Bird's campaign against the Kentucky fort at Ruddle's. Once the defenders opened the gates to lay down their arms, the warriors rushed in and began tomahawking and scalping everyone. Only with the greatest exertion of Captain Bird and his men were the lives of the bulk of the defenders saved, and then many of the women and children were taken by the Indians as captives. Since the burning of Crawford, every Rebel on the frontier knew what would happen to them if they fell into the hands of the Indians. No, the defenders at Weeling would fight to the death before they opened the gates to Indians, Caldwell reasoned, and it would be harder than hell to dislodge them in a frontal assault, which would result in many casualties. That was not the Indian and Ranger manner of waging war, Caldwell said. The Indians might have a chance attempting to burn one of the fort walls, but in the process, they would have to expose their warriors to the Shemanese rifles on the walls, which had greater range than Indian muskets, and

201

therefore could reach the warriors before any Rangers of Indians could hit them.

Simply, Caldwell argued that the lives of their warriors and his Rangers would be needlessly lost in attacking the fort. Caldwell couldn't see the point to it. The fort itself was too close to Rebel reinforcements from either Fort Pitt or the surrounding countryside to the east. Whereas, attacking Clark at the Falls of the Ohio made more sense to Caldwell. Clark had no way to get reinforcements or ammunition in the event that he was attacked over a period of days. Warriors could watch the trails coming from Kentucky and intercept any attempt to come to Clark's help. Whatever might come would have little strength. The Indians and his Rangers could take their time with Clark in wiping him out. Time would be on their side. Who might say that after having dealt decisively with Clark, that the Kentucky settlements could be destroyed completely as well. But an attack on Weeling held too many risks, one of which was leaving Clark active in their rear, which Caldwell did not like to think about. Clark would still be free to move, once the combined Indian and Ranger force left for Weeling. Caldwell summed up his argument by saying to the assembled chiefs that a decisive strike against the Shemanese captain Clark made much more sense to him. Weeling could wait until Detroit could supply them with an artillery piece.

However once Caldwell was finished, Captain Pipe began shaking his head in disagreement, which Caldwell could read correctly as stubborn disapproval. The Delaware chief was adamant. The Shemanese at Weel-lunk must be attacked now, before all else. The evil spirit there must be defeated and destroyed while the Indians had the strength to do it, regardless of the risks, or else that spirit, if allowed to remain, would come to cast its ill wind and dark clouds over all Indians in the Ohio Country, leading, ultimately, to their ruin. And so it was decided without further discussion. Captain Pipe pointed at Caldwell and put him on the spot. Would he and his men support the Delaware as they had supported him at the Upper Sandusky? Caldwell knew what the answer was before it was asked. In good faith he must support the Indians in their attack on Weeling, to the best of his ability, and that of his men. Yes, they would go to Weel-lunk, Caldwell said. However, the irony of the preceding argument was not lost on Caldwell, as the council broke up. He reflected on the number of times he had been in Pipe's place, arguing to the Iroquois in the Mohawk Valley that an attack could and should be made against a Rebel fort, only to have the Indians reluctant to do so, telling him it was not their way to make war by exposing themselves to needless casualties. Pipe's argument was entirely different, based upon ridding the Indians of an evil spirit to which end they appeared ready to sacrifice themselves. It was an argument that just didn't make sense to him any way that he looked at it.

Preparations for setting out on the path to Weel-lunk were made by mid-July. Indian runners were sent in all directions to every Indian village in the Ohio Country requesting all warriors. On the 12th of July, Alexander McKee, Captain of the British Indian Department in the Ohio Country, wrote Major DePeyster at Detroit, informing him of the decision of the Indians to attack Weeling. "Dear Sir, the 12th instant I joined Captain Caldwell at upper Sandusky, and after a few days consultation with the Indians collected there, we set off from thence towards Weeling, to strike the settlement of the Enemy." [146] The entire force consisted of over eleven hundred Indian warriors from a multitude of tribes and a full company of Butler's Rangers, along with a dozen white men of McKee's department. Caldwell had received a message in the interim from Detroit informing him that Bradt's company of Rangers was one their way to rendezvous with him either at the Shawnee village of Standing Stone or Piccawe. Apparently, Bradt did not know that Caldwell and the Indians were on the move.

Caldwell immediately sent a runner back to the lower Sandusky village to inform Bradt as to Caldwell's whereabouts, so that Bradt could join him with his men, at the first possible moment. Unknown to Caldwell, McKee, Bradt, or the Indians, Major DePeyster at Detroit had just received a shocking change of orders from Fort Niagara. DePeyster was stunned. Unbeknownst to him and anyone else in the Ohio Country, the war was apparently over. DePeyster wrote, "I dispatched an express to Captains Caldwell and Bradt, and one to Mr. Alexander McKee, ordering them not to make any incursions into the Enemy's Country, but to act on the defensive only. I hope the courier will be in time to stop Captain Bradt who is on the point of setting out for the neighborhood of Wheeling, but I fear Captain Caldwell has already passed the Ohio, in order to be satisfied of the enemies' motions, in which case he will strike some stroke before he returns." Yet disturbing reports continued to arrive at Detroit concerning the security of the post at Sandusky and the upper Indian villages. "I am informed by a deserter the enemy is determined to march, form one thousand to fifteen hundred strong. When the deserter left them, in the beginning of this month, the were assembling in the neighborhood of Wheeling and Fort McIntosh, under the command of the blood-thirsty Col. Williamson, who so much distinguished himself in the massacre of the Christian Indians at the settlement of Muskingum." [147] DePeyster hoped Caldwell and the Rangers could return at the first possible moment.

However, it was at this very moment when the Rangers and Indians had "advanced as far as the Whetstone branch of the Scioto between that place and Kooshawking," [148] wrote McKee, that fate intervened, or as the Delaware would have it, the evil spirit from Weel-lunk extended its long arm. "We were overtaken by a message from the Shawanese, informing us that their scouts were returned with a prisoner and scalp from the Falls [of the Ohio] who reports the enemy are assembled to come this way," wrote McKee to Detroit. Caldwell was more blunt in his assessment of what happened. "When I last had the pleasure of writing you I expected to have struck at Weeling as I was on my march for that place but was overtaken by a messenger from the Shawanese, who informed me the enemy was on their march for their country, which obliged me to turn their way, and to my great mortification, found the alarm false and that it was owing to a Gondal [large flat boat]coming up to the mouth of Licking Creek [on the Ohio River] and landing some men upon the south side of the Ohio, which when the Indians saw, supposed it was Clark." [149] What happened next was inexcusable as far as Caldwell was concerned. The Shawnee decided it most propitious that they return to their villages immediately, fearing that though the rumor of Clark's movement was proved to be false, nonetheless it foreshadowed to them that Clark would come anyway.

Caldwell was beside himself. The attack on either Weeling, or Kentucky, or the Falls of the Ohio was unraveling through no fault of his own, but because of the Indians. "I had eleven hundred Indians on the ground and three hundred within a day's march of me," wrote Caldwell, but it was all apparently for not. The largest body of Indian warriors ever assembled in the Ohio Country since the commencement of the war began to squabble, and that squabbling led to recriminations and distrust among them. The Shawnee, who were reluctant from the first to go to Weel-lunk at the insistence of the Delaware, were the first to leave. Said McKee, "When the return of the scouts from the Ohio informed us that the accounts we had received were false, this disappointment notwithstanding all our endeavors to keep them together occasioned them to disperse in disgust with each other. The inhabitants of this country who were the most immediately interested in keeping in a body were the first that broke off, and though we advanced towards the Ohio with upwards of three hundred Hurons and Lake Indians, few of the Delawares, Shawanese, or Mingos followed us." [150] It was a bitter pill for Caldwell and McKee to swallow. With the Delawares, Shawnee, and Mingos returning to Piccawe village [Piqua, Ohio], all that Caldwell could do was persuade the Wyandots and some Chippewa from Detroit, who were personally attached to him, to accompany him and the Rangers to attack the Virginians in Kentucky. McKee, Elliott, and Simon and George Girty, and the Indian department Frenchmen agreed to join the much smaller attack force. James Girty informed the rest that he would return with the Shawnee and Delaware to the upper villages and relay the message to Bradt and his Rangers when they arrived that Caldwell was one his way to Kentucky.

Chapter 15: At the Walls of White Man's Evil

The Delaware as a whole were in a very bad mood upon return to the mixed Shawnee village of Wapatomika. They and the Mingos would not speak to the Shawnee for their hand in derailing the attack against Weel-lunk, and went as far to accuse the Shawnee war captain, The Snake, of doing the bidding of the white man's evil spirit at Weel-lunk. Relations between the two tribes had never been at a lower point. However, the Delaware had borne some of the blame from Captain Caldwell for abandoning him after having him give his word to support them in the attack against Weel-lunk. Caldwell had been furious that the Delaware could abandon him so quickly. Morosely, they counseled with James Girty, the only white man present in camp of any standing with Caldwell, as to what they should do in light of what had happened. However, it was at this juncture, that The Great Spirit or the Evil Otkon altered the course of things. Captain Bradt of the Rangers with his company of forty men arrived at dusk from Sandusky with orders from Niagara to join Caldwell wherever he was. Immediately, the Delaware head men met privately to consider the possibility of convincing Bradt to accompany them to Weel-lunk to attack the Shemanese fort there.

In the morning, Captain Pipe and Wingemund met with Captain Bradt and James Girty. In an impassioned speech, Pipe exhorted the young Ranger captain to alter his orders and accompany the Delaware and Mingos on an attack on Weel-lunk. Pipe explained to Bradt that Caldwell had wanted to strike against the fort at Weel-lunk, and had set out with the Indians to do so. Unfortunately, he had been deceived by the

207

mischievous Shawnee who had given Caldwell a false report. They told him that Clark was marching with his army towards the Shawnee villages. Pipe said they did so in order that they could break off from Caldwell and the Delaware and abort the attack on Weel-lunk. As a result, Caldwell and his Rangers and the Wyandots crossed the Ohio River and headed south into Kan-tuck-ee. Pipe reasoned that by the time Bradt caught up with Caldwell, who was not on his way to Weel-lunk, Caldwell would have already struck a blow against the Shemanese to the south and would be on his way back. Pipe told Girty to tell the Ranger Captain that he knew Caldwell's mind, and that Caldwell would want Bradt to accompany the Delaware, Mingos and what few Shawnee and Wyandot warriors they could muster to attack the place that Caldwell had originally intended to do, which was of greater importance to the Delaware, and to Caldwell, than the Ken-tuck-ee settlements. If they were fortunate, and the Great Spirit favored them, they would be able to catch the fort's inhabitants by surprise as they were tending to their fields, and wipe them out and destroy the fort. Bradt would be back at Wapatomika about the same time Caldwell returned from Ken-tuck-ee, Pipe assured him.

New to the Ohio Country and the ways of the Indians there, Bradt could find no reason to oppose Pipe's request, and so gave his approval to join the war party. It was agreed that the force set out at the first possible moment. Pipe counseled separately with the Mingos and whatever Shawnee and Wyandot warriors who were left in the village. By the end of August, the combined war party of 238 Delaware, Mingo, Shawnee, and Wyandot warriors left for Weel-lunk with Bradt's thirty plus Rangers who were fit for duty, taking the path from the Scioto east to the former Delaware village of

Standing Stone, where they could follow a branch of the Mingo Path directly east to the creek that emptied into the Ohio River opposite to Weel-lunk, concealed in their approach by the island in the river there. Two days after the force left, a runner arrived at Wapatomika with DePeyster's dispatch for Caldwell and Bradt, ordering them both to refrain from any offensive action. It came too late to stop Bradt. The die had been cast for the attack on Weel-lunk. The force was considerably smaller than Pipe originally intended, but he was nonetheless optimistic that they would be successful in the endeavor that he had wished for from the beginning of the war—to eliminate Weel-lunk and its source of evil once and for all.

Things did not go well from the beginning for Pipe. Unfortunately, Caldwell's words came back to haunt him. The Indians were unable to catch the fort defenders outside the walls, nor could they plan for an ambush because Zane, in command of the fort, had indeed placed a scout across the Ohio River to keep watch over the Mingo Path, looking for Indian war parties, as Caldwell predicted Zane might do. From his lookout post on the fort wall overlooking the bluff of the river, Zane could see a horde of painted Indians crossing from the island at the shallows in the late afternoon of September 11th 1782. With them were a handful of white men too, which did not bode well to Zane. The recent arrival of John Linn had bought everyone enough time to save their lives but little else. The Indians had not caught the fifty or so men, women, and children out in the fields nor at their cabins or they would all be dead and scalped by now. Grabbing only their weapons, a little food, and their children, the settlers had rushed to the fort with no time to spare. Now, with the gates closed and almost three hundred Indians and their white allies beginning to surround Fort Henry at a distance, Zane realized his worst fear—this was not a small hit-and-run raid. The Indians were going to attack in force and were intent on destroying everyone and everything at Wheeling. Zane paused a moment and prayed to God to give him the courage to fight, and asking only for His salvation over all of their souls inside the fort, against the evil spirit of the Indians outside it.

Pipe was undeterred by the setback. He made his way with James Girty over to Bradt, and motioned to the Captain of the Rangers towards the fort, signaling to him that it was time for Bradt to call upon the defenders to surrender. Reluctantly, Bradt agreed, and sent Lieutenant Ferris forward with a white flag of truce attached to his musket. Soon, Ferris retraced his steps from the gates of Fort Henry to the spot where Captain Bradt and the company of Rangers lay concealed. Ferris tossed the flag aside and gave Bradt a nod, indicating the fort defenders were willing to listen to what he had to say. Bradt rose from his position and stood, studying the fort. There was no doubt in his mind that calling for their surrender was an exercise in futility; and one that might even get him shot. The Rebels would fight, he was sure of it, if Pipe wasn't. The Indians had seen to that when they showed the defenders their murderous intent while screaming hideous war whoops. Bradt knew that no one in their right mind would risk opening the gates to those savages. It had to be evident to the defenders that no matter what word he could give guaranteeing their safety, the Indians would never agree to it. The Rebels in the fort were outnumbered, but not stupid, and at the moment they held the upper hand.

Bradt had seen it before in the Mohawk Valley in New York. Once word of an impending raid reached a settlement, The Rebels holed up in their nearest fort, without engaging the raiders outside. The reason was

210

that forts were impregnable without artillery to batter down the gates. Any other attack would incur substantial casualties in the attempt. Casualties deep in enemy territory meant wounded Rangers would be left behind to the mercy of a vengeful enemy. Consequently, without artillery, the point was not to directly attack the frontier fort, but rather scorch the earth around it, leaving no food or shelter standing for the Rebels, once the Rangers moved on. Any other strategy was foolish, such as what Pipe and the Delaware were proposing. Bradt implicitly understood that all the Rebels in the fort needed to do was hold out till reinforcements arrived or the Indians lost interest. They would win by not needing to defeat the Rangers and Indians in the open. Still, Bradt reminded himself that he had to mollify Captain Pipe and the Delaware, or face their wrath. Girty had told him that Pipe still believed that the defenders would open the gates when Bradt ordered them to do so.

Bradt motioned for privates Larraway, Johnson, and West to accompany him as a guard to the parley. Corporal Vrooman would carry the British flag; Lieutenant Ferris would remain in command of the rest of the men in case something went wrong. [151] With everything ready, they set out across the 150 yards to the fort, with Captain Bradt leading the way. It was not without trepidation, for Bradt knew the Rebels could just as easily shoot him down in front of the fort as to talk to him. He had come a long way since leaving his home near Johnstown, New York, in 1777 to die at this wilderness fort. It had been six long years of constant warfare, Bradt reflected, as he and his party closed the distance to the fort walls. The Ranger company had dwindled to little more than thirty men due to attrition and a lack of recruits. Rumors at Niagara were circulating when Bradt and his men left for Sandusky that the war was lost for the King in the East. If so, the best thing he could do for his men was to get them safely back to Canada and reunite them with their families, once hostilities ceased. To that end he would help the Indians as best he could, without exposing his men to a costly frontal assault on the fort. Reaching the fort, Bradt called on the Rebel commander to surrender, who told him to wait for a response. It wasn't long in coming. Without further word, the officer fired his wall swivel gun over Bradt's head. The battle of futility had officially begun.

James Girty threw more wood on the council fire, as he watched the expressions of the Indian war captains sitting across from him. Girty listened carefully as each man spoke his turn. Though Girty was sure that they could be seen from the blockhouse outside the fort, with darkness approaching, the war council was out of gunshot range. Girty listened without interrupting. He understood every word without explanation. At the moment, the headmen were angry with Pipe and Bradt that the fort had not fallen by surprise, ambush, or surrender. Girty knew that it was not his place to speak at this council without causing offense. Holding his tongue was a lesson of protocol that he learned from his brother Simon. As an interpreter, he understood he must let a chief speak until he had finished, and not offer an opinion to the Indians unless asked. These war captains had led the attack on the Virginians and not James or Simon, as the Rebels believed. Nor was the ranger captain Bradt in command of the Indians. Girty was there to repeat what the chiefs said if they wished Bradt to know. As a sworn interpreter he would do so honestly and truthfully, never violating the trust placed in him by the Indians.

Girty gazed into the fire as the headmen talked. He remembered when he and his brothers and their mother sat before a similar fire years ago, as Delaware argued the fate of his step-father John Turner. They had been captured from their home by a French and Indian war party in Pennsylvania in 1756, and taken to the village of Kittanning above the Forks of the Ohio. The boys witnessed Turner slowly burned to death to satisfy Indian vengeance. This past spring, James had witnessed Crawford die by fire to avenge the Delaware deaths of women and children at Gnadenhutten. Even though Crawford had not taken part in the killing of the Christian Indians, he had brought his army to the Upper Sandusky with murderous intent. For that, Crawford must die. Girty could understand that. With the Indians, just like the white preachers, an "eye for an eye" was the teaching of their own God. After the death of Turner, James had been sent across the river deep into the Ohio Country to be adopted by the Shawnee, who took him to their towns on the Scioto River, where a family accepted him as a son once his "white blood" was washed away.

Those years living with the Shawnee were the happiest time of his life. James learned their customs, language, and woodland skills, and was treated with respect as an equal by all. However that came to an end when the new peace with the whites demanded that all white captives be repatriated. James was reunited with his brothers at Fort Pitt, but all did not go well. At twenty, he could not speak or understand English. He was met by the settlers there will cold malevolent stares. They called him "Injun Girty" and a "white Indian," meaning, someone who had lived too many years with the savages. Even the Christian preacher went as far to say that James had the red devil inside of him. James could not fit into frontier society, with his broken English and Indian ways. He was treated as an outcast, and worked by hunting for the fort commander, and translating when the Shawnee came to trade during the years of peace. In time, James worked for Alexander McKee and Matthew Elliott who were traders to the Indians and traveled to their villages in the Ohio Country. James was able to frequently return to the home of his adopted people. So it was an easy decision to flee Pittsburgh when war broke out and return to the Shawnee, whom he truly missed. In his heart and mind, James considered himself Shawnee, and would always remain so, but there were times when he was conflicted, and this was one of them.

In the upper tier of the blockhouse, Ebenezer Zane peered out of the gun port, towards the fire he could see in the distance to the south of the fort, out of gunshot range. The Indians were up to something, he figured. They must be counseling as to what to do next, now that that their hope to ambush the fort, or call for its surrender hadn't got them anywhere. The whites with them would be giving them ideas, Zane guessed, but his gut told him that they might not be leading the attack. They had not shown themselves since the flag of truce, and had no artillery with them, or they already would have made a show of it, and blasted the gates open, which the Indians would have immediately forced them to do. No, this attack was different than anything Zane had ever seen or heard of before. Indians attacking a fort, and acting like they intended to stay at it sounded personal to him. For the life of him, Zane couldn't understand it. It was if the Indians had a bone to pick with him and his family personally, which didn't make sense. Zane had steered clear of Williamson and Crawford, choosing not to take part in their expeditions against the hostiles. Besides, Ebenezer had a brother, Isaac, living with the Wyandot in the Ohio Country as an adopted son. Certainly Isaac would have got word to him if the Indians had some particular blood feud with him. Regardless of whatever reason, Zane forced himself to review the things that had gone right up to this point. He had done right by having Linn out scouting on the Indian path across the Ohio to warn them if a war party approached. It worked. And the blockhouse had been key in keeping the Indians hunkered down from their rifle fire that covered most parts of the fort walls and the ground leading up to it. Most of all, Zane had been able to get a rider headed east towards Catfish Camp, and reinforcements. All they needed to do now was to hold out until either help arrived, or the Indians got tired of the whole thing and faded away as they were known to do, and which Zane hoped would happen.

Yet, Zane was troubled. He realized there was something more he needed to do that he had been neglectful of. Zane had not prayed for God's help, and so he got down on his knees, and baring his head, began to do so. Zane considered himself a God-fearing man, and had tried to live his life according to the Good Book, even though he realized at times he failed at it, and failed God. He felt shortcomings in God's eyes had now come back to haunt him, so with clasped hands, Zane prayed to the Lord as he had never done before, asking salvation not for himself, but for his family and friends inside the blockhouse and the fort. He told the Lord that they were good God-fearing people who had placed their trust in Zane, and had followed him here to this place Zane called his vision of paradise. Now, all that they had done to make this place their home was in jeopardy. The Indians wanted to do more than just destroy it. They wanted everyone's flesh and blood as well; some sort of personal vengeance. So Zane prayed for forgiveness of his sins, and asked the Lord God to see him through this trial the Lord had put before him to test his own faith. Too, Zane prayed that God would give him the strength and courage to be the instrument of His will, and to do whatever He wished with Zane, even if it meant

215

sacrificing his life so that the others could be saved. Zane asked God to make him His sword to smite the Heathen in the wilderness who had evil in their hearts, as Zane seen it. With that, the prayer was over.

Standing up, Zane cleared his head, and put his tricorn back on. It was time to let his thinking mind take over, as he was confident the Lord would approve of. A man like Zane had learned to live and survive on the frontier by using his wits in addition to his faith. The Lord would help those who helped themselves, Zane told others in times of crisis, and now was no time to lose their heads and forsake common sense and logic. Zane's instincts told him he must out-think the Indians so as to take the initiative away from them, and make them react to him, rather than being caught off guard by their guile. What would the Indians do next, he asked himself? What would he do if he was in their place outside the walls trying to get in? As his mind pondered the question, Zane reviewed again what had happened after the call for surrender had been rebuffed. No cannon had been forthcoming, meaning, they had none. The Indians had not committed to an assault on the fort because Zane and the others in the blockhouse had forced them to keep their heads down. The field of fire from the blockhouse had been the key. That was it; that was the answer Zane was looking for. The Indians would next try to eliminate the blockhouse. They would wait for the cover of darkness so they could not be seen, and shot at. The only way they could destroy the blockhouse without having cannon was to attempt to burn it down. Yes, Zane told himself, an attack was coming as soon as darkness fell. The Indians would creep up to the blockhouse with combustibles and firebrands. Hastily, Zane barked to the others with him to draw buckets of water from the well. They were soon going to need it.

Back in the Indian camp, Girty listened to the council. Pipe had brought with him an old Delaware chief to speak. The aged Indian, stooped by his years, arose from the throng of over two hundred warriors now gathered around the council fire. He began, speaking slowly in the Delaware tongue so that the Wyandot, Shawnee, and Mingo could comprehend what he had to say. The old chief had been an orator, who was born in the Delaware village of Shannopin's Town, and had lived most of his years at Goschachgunk. He now recounted the history of this place to which the Indians had come, sworn to exact revenge. "Brothers! Listen to me...Look about you. We Delaware people call this Weel-lunk, Place of the Skull. It is hard to imagine that this land was once a beautiful place; Delaware land given to us by the Great Spirit to live upon, and uphold. The forest stood tall; the soil rich and unblemished; the waters clear. Bountiful were elk, deer, bear, beaver, and otter. Since I was a child, our people camp here to camp and hunt, as our Fathers, the Iroquois had done. It was here that we prepared food for winter and to take many skins to trade with the English who came from across the mountains. Children were born here. The bones of many of our ancestors sleep beneath our feet. This land you see next to the great river, O-Yee-O was held in the hearts of our people as dear to us. Now it is a place of bad blood, of suffering, and sorrow, and sadness for the Iroquois and all Delaware. It is a place cursed to all Indians by the whites."

The old man continued his oratory, his wrinkled face illuminated in the flickering light of the fire's flames. "Like an ill wind, first the English rum traders came from across the mountains in the east to prey upon us. They stole our furs and gave us liquor that drove our young men mad. They abused our women and even spilled Delaware blood. The head placed upon the pole here at the mouth of the creek was a white man's head, that of a rum trader. It served to satisfy Indian vengeance, and cleanse this place of the evil that took place here. But the evil of the white man only attracted more evil. First, the Frenchman Celeron came here and told Indians that his French Father across the great water wanted this land for his own. Then an English man named Gist told us that his father from Virginia over the mountains wanted the land for the English King. Did they think this Indian land was empty land? When the English defeated the French, they called themselves masters of all Indian lands, allowing the Shemanese to come across the mountains, mad with lust for our land. Here, Zane and his brothers fell trees and break soil, and call it their own. We kept our hatchets buried, and restrained our young men until the outrages have become too much.

Cresap, Clark and Williamson have come from Weel-lunk. Williamson is the murderer of our innocent people. He and his men crushed their skulls, took their scalps, and threw their bodies in a heap upon a fire, some still alive at the Moravian village. This loss had been more than our broken hearts can bear. I call upon the Great Spirit that rules this entire world to give us the strength to rid this place of the white man's evil that has come to reside here, that has been so injurious to our people. Many of our hatchets are yet shiny after the defeat of the army of Crawford who came with his men to kill even more of us at the Upper Sandusky. Yet the spirits of our innocent cry out for vengeance to be fulfilled. Oh Great Spirit! We ask you to give us strength and courage to be the instrument of that vengeance. The blood of our murdered women and children begs to be paid for with the blood of the whites here at Weel-lunk, the center of their evil. Only then can we cleanse this place and forsake the name that evil has marked it by. Only then can the Lenape rest."

    James Girty's mind became troubled as he listened to the old Delaware chief, and he did not know why. Implicitly he understood the orator's message that was coming from his heart, and that was striking a sympathetic chord in Girty. Girty knew the truth of what the old man was saying because Girty thought like an Indian as he knew himself to be. Alexander McKee, who had a white mother who had been captured by the Shawnee as a child, once told Girty that because his thoughts were created in the Indian language that he had an Indian mind in a white body, like McKee's mother. This was evident to Girty by his difficulty in re-learning the English words when he was returned to the whites at Pittsburgh at the end of the wars. This meant that Girty could see the world as the Indians do, could understand what they understood, and know the evil spirits that resided at Weel-lunk without having to be there. Girty's Indian mind allowed him to feel the evil; smell it, and be aware of its presence and power. But it was something else that Girty was aware of that troubled him at times; that he couldn't explain. Something inside of him was aware of his Indian mind; was watching his Indian thoughts in times of strain and stress such as this. McKee told him that his mother said that beneath the outer Indian mind of a child captive lay a mostly silent inner mind; the white mind that he was born with, that had not been washed away at the time of his adoption. It was a sentience that had not been replaced by the world created by the Shawnee language. Girty recognized that it was that sentience that was speaking to him now, in whispers, even as he was aware of his Indian mind straining to shut it out.

The sentience began when the old Delaware chief beseeched the Great Spirit for help. It made Girty think of the white preachers he had seen and heard at Pittsburgh doing a similar thing. He recalled in particular the preacher David McClure who came to minister to the Shawnee on the Scioto. McClure told them that he brought with him his White God, and asked the Indians to pray with him to this God, by beseeching the God's attention. The Shawnee had no interest in this new God and banished McClure from their village. The lingering memory of his preaching is what triggered the inner whisper inside Girty. "Are there two Great Spirits in the heavens doing battle with each other, one White and one Red?" the voice whispered. "Or are they two faces of the same God; each face appearing evil to the other? Is it the same God that looks upon one people with one face, finding fault with the other people and listing grievances, and seeking revenge on the other, and the other face likewise doing the same? Does one face call Weel-lunk a vision of paradise, and the other call it a place of evil? How has this One Spirit become one with two faces that are both good and both evil; both right and both wrong; both wishing to see their own people prosper and wishing the other's to suffer and die," the voiced whispered? "Are the two faces but a single reflection, seen in the water two different ways by man—whites the one way, and Indians the other?" Girty quietly stood up as the chief continued to exhort the warriors. The quandary he found himself in had reached a point that he could endure it no longer. There were no answers to the questions posed by the whispers; only more questions and Girty had had enough of it.

It was at that moment that Pipe called to Girty. The Indians had decided to attack the Shemanese blockhouse once the moon set. Pipe wanted Girty to relay their decision to the ranger captain Bradt, so that he could order his men to help in the attack with covering fire. Soon, warriors under the cover of darkness crept up to the blockhouse and attempted to set fire to it with firebrands, to try to eliminate the source of the rifle-fire that was covering any direct approach to the fort. Time and time again throughout the fitful night the Indian attempts to burn it out, and then the fort itself, were repulsed with gunfire and buckets of water thrown from the gun ports upon the kindling fires. The nighttime attacks left the defenders exhausted. Dawn brought a resumption of shooting by the Indians and Rangers, but with no lasting effect. The Indians next attempted to fire a hand-made wooden cannon at the fort gates. It had been fashioned from a hollowed out log wrapped in chains, but failed to work, which heartened the fort defenders. However, an unexpected crisis arose in the fort in the afternoon. Silas Zane, brother of Ebenezer, discovered the fort's supply of gunpowder had almost run out.

During the initial rush to get everyone inside the fort before the Indians attacked, the gunpowder stored in the blockhouse had not been brought over to the fort. Among the defenders, Elizabeth "Betty" Zane, sister of the Zane brothers, volunteered to run to the blockhouse and bring back gunpowder to the fort, telling everyone that she would not be missed as much as man shooting on the wall of the fort, if killed. Fleet of foot, Betty dashed to the blockhouse unmolested during a lull in the battle. Bradt had noticed it peculiar that the shots from the fort were noticeably slacking just prior to Betty's run, and guessed correctly that the fort was running low on ammunition when he spied the young woman burst from the fort gates and sprint to the blockhouse. He motioned to Pipe and the warriors to be on guard; that the woman was likely to run back to the fort soon. So on her return with a load of gunpowder in her apron, bullets

221

whizzed around her as the Indians and Rangers attempted to bring her down, yelling to each other, "Squaw! Squaw!" Luckily, Betty made it safely back to the fort unscathed, and soon a brisk return fire from the fort resumed.

The siege continued unabated into the night with several more attempts made by the Indians to burn the fort palisades from different sides. All were repulsed by the defenders. The strain of constant fighting combined with dread, thirst, hunger, and sleeplessness was taking its toll on those inside the fort and blockhouse, as was written on everyone's faces. Those hours till dawn of the third day of the siege were the worst that anyone who lived through it would later remember. The smoke from the burning cabins mingling with the cries of babies, the sobbing of the youngest children, the moans of the wounded; and the distant shrieks of the Indians were almost more than anyone could bear. Still, they held out, and prayed. As the sky lightened in the east, the defenders found most of the Indians gone, with some spied from the fort walls to be crossing the river to the island at the shallows, headed west. It was a cautious moment for rejoicing. However, everyone could see from the walls their devastated homes and slaughtered livestock laying everywhere. Not daring to leave the fort or the blockhouse for fear of an Indian ambush, Zane realized that the battle was truly over when a mounted relief force from Catfish Camp arrived around noon. He knew they could now open the gates and give thanks to the Lord for their salvation, which they had fought for. God had truly helped those who helped themselves fight for their lives with dogged determination and raw courage not to give up or give in.

From a vantage point on the island, James Girty paused for a moment to take a last look at Weel-lunk, guessing to himself that he would not see it again. Captain Pipe and a handful of warriors who were the last to cross at the shallow, came up to Girty. "So many things of the white man's evil at Place of the Skull thwarted us and the power of the Great Spirit," lamented Pipe. "The scout who spied us, the refusal to surrender, the cannon that would not work, the water to quench the firebrands, the white squaw's run...." Pipe's voice trailed off. "It was the work of the Great Evil here. Too much evil. Too much evil power at Place of the Skull. We will not get another chance," Pipe said as he turned his back on Weel-lunk. Girty, who had been listening in silence and nodding his head in agreement with Pipe, turned again for a last glimpse. "Too much evil here?" Girty reflected. "No cannon," came a whisper.

The voice inside him was like a murmuring wind now.

"Battle lost, war lost, land lost, way of life lost."

There was silence, and then it whispered a last time, as if to sum up.

"It began at Weel-lunk, foretold by a head on a post, at the Place of the Skull."

Girty shrugged his shoulders and adjusted his pack. The voice was gone and his thoughts were no longer on Weel-lunk and the past, but rather focused on the image of his wife and child at their village on the Scioto, where he was intent on making his way.

Place of the Skull

224

Chapter 16: Aftermath

The second siege of Fort Henry, fought on September 11th, 12th, and 13th 1782, was a pivotal moment for everyone involved. It became known as the Last Battle of the American Revolution by historians because it was the last time in the long war for American independence that British military forces engaged Americans, in this case, Virginian militiamen. The handful of Virginians under Ebenezer Zane and his brother Silas were successful in their defense of the fort. It was the last time that Wheeling was attacked by Indians, though isolated war parties sporadically raided the east side of the Ohio River around Wheeling for several years after the battle. In the years to come, the defenders of Fort Henry went on to establish Wheeling as a key hub of commerce and fledgling industry, and an important transportation point for river traffic headed down the Ohio River for destinations in southern Ohio and the Kentucky lands that were increasingly opening up for settlement. By the turn of the century, Ebenezer Zane petitioned the government for funds to open the Indian Mingo Path that headed west from Wheeling into a road which eventually became the National Road.

William Caldwell, his company of Rangers, and the Lake Indians with him, were not able to destroy the Kentucky fort called Bryant's Station, due to a similar lack of artillery. However, Caldwell was able to draw the Kentucky militiaman relief force into an ambush at Blue Licks with great success. Upon returning with Bradt's company to the Upper Sandusky Indian villages, Caldwell found orders waiting for him and Bradt to return with their men to Fort Niagara and cease all military offensive actions against the American frontier. The war was effectively over, and the corps of Butler's

Rangers were soon to be disbanded. Unfortunately for them, they were unable to return to their former homes in the new United States of America, due to their service in the war as a loyalist unit fighting alongside the Indians across the breadth of the American frontier. Consequently, men like Caldwell and Bradt took their families to Canada, where they began a new life along with men from other former loyalist military units.

For the Indians, the end of the battle at Weellunk signaled many things. Losing the battle meant that the British and Indians had lost the war. For the Indians, that was tragic. Their attempt to drive out the white settlers from their lands in the Ohio Country had failed, and with the peace, came the prospect that a flood of new white settlers would invade the Indian lands. However, the repercussion of the peace between Great Britain and the United States devastated the Indian tribes as a whole when they discovered, to their shock, that Great Britain had ceded all the lands south of the Great Lakes and west of the Allegheny Mountains to the Americans, as one of the terms of the peace. Not only had the British agreed to hand over the Indian lands to the Americans, it had been done so without consulting the Indians whatsoever. They had been intentionally written out of the treaty terms, and now discovered themselves to be sold out to their hated former enemies. Losing their lands meant that their former traditional way of life was lost.

Joseph Brant, war captain of the Mohawks, traveled to British Headquarters in Quebec to express his shock and dismay on May 21, 1783, to General Haldimand, Commander-in-Chief of British forces in the Northern Department. "Wherefore Brother I am now sent in behalf of all the King's Indian Allies to receive a decisive Answer from You, and to know, Whether they are included in this Treaty with the Americans as faithful Allies should be, or not? And whether those Lands which the Great Being above has pointed out for our Ancestors and their Descendants, and placed them there from the beginning and where the Bones of our forefathers are Laid is secured to them? Or whether the Blood of their grandchildren is to be mingled with their Bones, through the means of our Allies for whom We have often so freely Bled?" [152] Brant did not receive a reply from Haldimand, because he had none. There was nothing he could say to Brant and the British Indian allies who had served the British cause in war and were now abandoned with the peace terms. The Indians were forced to give up their homes and villages in the Ohio Country to the Americans over succeeding years, so that by the early 1800's there were no more Shawnee, Mingo, Wyandot, and Delaware Indians living on the land that they had formerly called their own.

There was an irony following the defeat of the Indians at Wheeling for Ebenezer Zane. With the end of the war, he could have named the young settlement at Fort Henry that he had been instrumental in establishing, after himself, as most prominent settlers were apt to do. Wheeling, an Indian word and a place name, would likely have become Zanesburg, Zanestown, Zanesville, or Zaneton. Ebenezer Zane chose not to do so for whatever reason that was never expressed or recorded. He kept the Delaware name for the spot, Weel-lunk, which became pronounced and spelled in English as Wheeling in the years thereafter the war, choosing the Indian name for the place Zane was reported to have called, "a vision of Paradise," when he first set eyes on it. [153] Few white settlers to Wheeling in succeeding years and generations to follow would ever know the Indian meaning of the name that meant Place of the Skull.

Why did Zane choose not to change the name? Perhaps he was as cautious about changing an Indian name as he had been about fighting Indians, knowing to always be on your guard, and never have disrespect for the unexpected. Zane knew the story that the Indian name Weel-lunk meant Place of the Skull. He would have understood that something of significance to Indians had happened years before he came to the place; something which they Indians considered bad enough to put a white man's skull upon a pole to mark the place so no Indian would forget. Zane might have been superstitious about the presence of evil Indian spirits. In spite of his own religion to bolster his faith in a Christian God, Zane had spent a lifetime on the Indian frontier. He was a survivor of many an Indian war party and skirmish. While others had died at the hands of the Indians, Zane, due to his overly-cautious nature, had lived. If he had learned anything about dealing with Indians, it was to never allow himself to let his guard down, or turn his back to them. Perhaps he felt the same way about their belief in evil spirits.

In the end, Zane thought it wise to leave the Indian name alone, as the Indians wished, so as to not disturb whatever it was that Indians had ascribed to the Place of the Skull that he did not know, nor want to know of. And so it remains today; one of the few cities in the United States that has kept its Indian name, and the only place where that Indian name means, "Place of the Skull." It is what the Indians desired two hundred and seventy years ago. Wheeling: The place of white man's evil towards Indians—"Place of the Skull."

Acknowledgements

Noted Wheeling historian and archivist Margaret Brennan was instrumental in providing me with the inspiration for writing this book. We had, on several occasions, spirited discussions of Wheeling's earliest history and the mystery surrounding how Wheeling got its name and for what reasons. This led me to question the reliability of the earliest story told to the Zanes by Delaware Indians, which has been accepted since 1769 as truth, which I began to question. Margaret pointed me in the right direction in Wheeling's archives, and to the original research done by historian Delf Norona in 1948 on the same subject. Without Margaret's help, the impetus to write this book would not have arisen, and to her I am deeply grateful.

I am deeply indebted to Cecy Rose for the enormous amount of effort that she committed to this project to see it through to its fruition on many levels. In the beginning, Cecy served as a sounding board for my initial outline of the book, and aided me in shaping my ideas into something that she thought might be readable. As an accomplished Wheeling area artist, Cecy was able to create the cover oil painting, "Place of the Skull" for the book from my historical perspective of what such an image might appear like as described sparsely in the 18th Century historical record. In addition, Cecy's digital computer skills in formatting the text into printable form from beginning to end were simply beyond the scope of my abilities as a writer. In all, Cecy's help was invaluable and to her I wish to extend my heart-felt gratitude for all that she has done to make this possible.

Place of the Skull

Bibliography

Blumel, Benjamin, The Zanes: A Frontier Family, iUniverse, Lincoln, NE, 2005.

Bonaparte, Darren, A Lily Among Thorns, The Wampum Chronicles, Ahkwesahsne Mohawk Territory, NY, 2009.

Crytzer, Brady, Fort Pitt, A Frontier History, The History Press, Charleston, SC, 2012.

Crytzer, Brady, Guyasuta, Westholme Publishing, Yardley, Pennsylvania, 2013.

Darlington, William, Christopher Gist's Journals, Heritage Books, Westminster, Maryland, 2006.

Donehoo, George, Indian Villages and Place Names in Pennsylvania, Wennawoods, Lewisburg, PA, 1998.

Downes, Randolph, Council Fires on the Upper Ohio, University of Pittsburgh Press, Pittsburgh, PA, 1940.

Fitzpatrick, Alan, Wilderness War on the Ohio, Fort Henry Publications, Benwood, WV, 2003.

Fitzpatrick, Alan, In Their Own Words, Fort Henry Publications, Benwood, WV, 2009

Friederici, Georg, Scalping in America, Iroqrafts, Ohsweken, Ontario, 1985.

Hanna, Charles, The Wilderness Trail, G.P. Putnam's Sons, NY, NY, 1911.

Hartley, Cecil, Lewis Wetzel, The Virginia Ranger, Evans Publisher, Philadelphia, PA, 1860.

Heckewelder, John, History, Manners, and Customs of the Indian Nations, Ayre Publishers, N. Stratford, NH, 2005.

Hurt, R. Douglas, The Ohio Frontier, Indiana University Press, Bloomington, Indiana, 1996.

Knowles, Nathaniel, The torture of Captives by the Indians, Iroqrafts, Ohsweken, Ontario, 1985.

Kummerow, O'Toole, and Stephenson, Forbes Trail, Taylor Trade Publishing, NY, 2008.

McDonough, Joseph, Joutel's Journal of la Salle's Last Voyage, Albany, NY, 1906.

Moorehead, William King, The Indian Tribes of Ohio, Smoke and Fire Co., Waterford, Ohio 1899 reprint.

Norona, Delf, Wheeling: A West Virginia Place-Name of Indian Origin, unpublished, Wheeling, WV, 1958.

Parkman, Francis, La Salle and the Discovery of the Great West, Boston: Little, Brown, 1869.

Shannon, Timothy, Iroquois Diplomacy on the Early American Frontier, Penguin Books, NY, 2008.

Spencer, C. Allan, They Gave the Scalp Halloo, Studitchulon Press, Wheeling, WV 2013.

Volwiler, Albert, George Croghan, Wennawoods Publishing, Lewisburg, PA, 2000.

Wallace, Paul, Conrad Weiser, Wennawoods Publishing, Lewisburg, PA, 1996.

Wallace, Paul, Indians in Pennsylvania, PA Historical and Museum Commission, Harrisburg, PA, 1993.

Wallace, Paul, Indian Paths of Pennsylvania, PA Historical and Museum Commission, Harrisburg, PA, 1998.

Wallace, Paul, Thirty Thousand Miles with John Heckewelder, Wennawoods Publishing, Lewisburg, PA, 1998.

Wilcox, Frank, Ohio Indian Trails, Gates Press, Cleveland, Ohio, 1933.

Withers, Alexander, Chronicles of Border Warfare, McClain Printing, Parsons, WV, 1961.

Zeisberger, David, History of the North American Indians, Wennawoods Publishing, Lewisburg, PA, 1999.

References

[1] Parkman, Francis, La Salle and the Discovery of the Great West, Boston: Little, Brown, 1869.

[2] Moorehead, William King, The Indian Tribes of Ohio, page 14.

[3] Joutel, Henri, Joutel's Journal of La Salle's Last Voyage, 1684-7, page 225.

[4] Moorehead, The Indian Tribes of Ohio, page 14.

[5] Wallace, Paul A.W., Indian Paths of Pennsylvania, #64. The Mingo Path, page 100.

[6] Wallace, ibid, page 100.

[7] Blumel, Benjamin, The Zanes: A Frontier Family, page 85.

[8] Shannon, Timothy, Iroquois Diplomacy of the Early American Frontier, page 26.

[9] Bonaparte, Darren, A Lily Among Thorns, page 28.

[10] Spencer, C. Allan, They Gave the Scalp Halloo, page 158.

[11] Spencer, ibid, page 159.

[12] Bonaparte, Darren, A Lily Among Thorns, page 62.

[13] Wikipedia.org/wiki/Iroquois, "Food."

[14] Spencer, They Gave the Scalp Halloo, page 59.

[15] Spencer, ibid, page 58.

[16] Spencer, ibid, page 71.

[17] Knowles, Nathaniel, Torture of Captives by Indians, page 70.

[18] Heckewelder, John, History, Manners and Customs of the Indian Nations Who Once Inhabited Pennsylvania and the Neighboring States, page 173.

[19] Spencer, They Gave the Scalp Halloo, page1.

[20] Spencer, ibid, page 2.

[21] Heckewelder, John, History, Manners and Customs, page 175.

[22] Heckewelder, ibid, page 175.

[23] Spencer, They Gave the Scalp Halloo, page 2.

Place of the Skull

[24] Spencer, ibid, page 9.
[25] Spencer, ibid, page 9.
[26] Bonaparte, A Lily Among Thorns, page 36.
[27] Federici, Georg, Scalping in America, page 3.
[28] Bonaparte, A Lily Among Thorns, pages 38-41.
[29] Shannon, Iroquois Diplomacy, page 32.
[30] Wikipedia.org/wiki/Beaver Wars.
[31] Bonaparte, A Lily Among Thorns, page 57.
[32] Moorehead, Indian Tribes of Ohio, page 4.
[33] Moorehead, ibid, page 4.
[34] Bonaparte, A Lily Among Thorns, page 102.
[35] Bonaparte, page 112-113.
[36] Shannon, Iroquois Diplomacy, page 41.
[37] Shannon, ibid, page 41-42.
[38] Donehoo, George, Indian Villages and Place Names in Pennsylvania, page 14.
[39] Donehoo, ibid, page 100.
[40] Donehoo, ibid, page 83.
[41] Donehoo, ibid, page 167.
[42] Donehoo, ibid, page 190.
[43] Donehoo, ibid, page 93.
[44] Hanna, Charles, The Wilderness Trail, page 316.
[45] Donehoo, Indian Villages and Place Names, page 108.
[46] Wallace, Indians of Pennsylvania, page 12.
[47] Hanna, Charles, The Wilderness Trail, page 143.
[48] Donehoo, Indian Villages and Place Names, page 134.
[49] Donehoo, ibid, page 92.
[50] Hanna, Charles, the Wilderness Trail, page 143.
[51] Donehoo, Indian Villages and Place Names, page 92.
[52] Hanna, The Wilderness Trail, page 170.
[53] Donehoo, Indian Villages and Place Names, page 67.
[54] Donehoo, ibid, page 67.
[55] Donehoo, ibid, page 67.
[56] Hanna, The Wilderness Trail, page 174.

234

[57] Hanna, ibid, page 163.
[58] Wallace, Paul, Friend of Colonist and Mohawk, page 21.
[59] Wallace, ibid, page 371.
[60] Wallace, ibid, page 485.
[61] Donehoo, Indian Villages and Place Names, page 190.
[62] Downes, Randolph, Council Fires on the Upper Ohio, page 25.
[63] Downes, ibid, page 21.
[64] Downes, ibid, page 21.
[65] Downes, ibid, page 21.
[66] Downes, ibid, page 22.
[67] Downes, ibid, page 23.
[68] Downes, ibid, page 31.
[69] Downes, ibid, page 32.
[70] Hanna, The Wilderness Trail, page 309
[71] Wallace, Friend of Colonist and Mohawk, page 42.
[72] Hanna, ibid, page 287.
[73] Hanna, ibid, page 287.
[74] Downes, ibid, page 34.
[75] Hanna, The Wilderness Trail, page 306.
[76] Hanna, ibid, page 306.
[77] Colonial Records of Pennsylvania, Volume 4, page 470.
[78] Colonial Records of Pennsylvania, Volume 4, page 656.
[79] Donehoo, Indian Villages and Place Names, page 22.
[80] Colonial Records of Pennsylvania, Volume 4, page 656.
[81] Wallace, Conrad Weiser, pages 266, 269.
[82] Heckewelder, John, History, Manners, and Customs of the Indian Nations, page 328.
[83] Heckewelder, ibid, page 328.
[84] Wallace, Paul, Conrad Weiser, page 21.
[85] Wallace, ibid, page 88.

[86] Mieder, Wolfgang, The Only Good Indian is a Dead Indian: History and Meaning of a Proverbial Stereotype, Journal of American Folklore, Volume 106, No. 419.

[87] Heckewelder, History, Manners, and Customs of the Indian Nations, page 334.

[88] The Bible, Exodus, Chapter 21, Verse 24.

[89] Heckewelder, History, Manners and Customs of the Indian Nations, page 332.

[90] Donehoo, Indian Villages and Place Names, page 251.

[91] Norona, Delf, Wheeling, West Virginia Place Name, page 6.

[92] Norona, ibid, page 2.

[93] Norona, ibid, page 3.

[94] Norona, ibid page 6-7.

[95] Norona, ibid, page 29.

[96] Darlington, William, Christopher Gist's Journals, page 77.

[97] Norona, Delf, Wheeling West Virginia Place Name, page 29.

[98] Darlington, ibid, page 77.

[99] Parkman, Francis, Montcalm and Wolfe, page 457.

[100] Brumwell, Stephen, White Devil, page 201.

[101] Fitzpatrick, Alan, Wilderness War on the Ohio, page 297-298.

[102] Heckewelder, History, Manners, and Customs of the Indian Nations, pages 329, 332.

[103] Fitzpatrick, Wilderness War on the Ohio, page 490.

[104] Heckewelder, History, Manners and Customs of the Indian Nations, pages 287-288.

[105] Wallace, Paul, Indians in Pennsylvania, page 67.

[106] Wallace, ibid, page 68.

[107] Zeisberger, David, History of the Northern American Indians, page 131.

[108] Wallace, ibid, page 70.

[109] Wallace, ibid, page 69.

[110] Wallace, ibid, page 77.

[111] Zeisberger, History of the Northern American Indians, page 89.

[112] www.trueghosttales.com/native-americans-ghosts-and-evil-spirits, Native Americans and Ghosts and Evil Spirits

[113] Dennis, Matthew, American Indians, Witchcraft, and Witch-Hunting, Magazine of History, Vol. 17, No. 4, July 2003.

[114] Wallace, Paul, Conrad Weiser, page 82.

[115] Dennis, American Indians, Witchcraft, and Witch-Hunting.

[116] Wallace, Conrad Weiser, page 82.

[117] Wallace, Indians in Pennsylvania, page 177.

[118] Wallace, ibid, page 177.

[119] Wallace, Paul, Conrad Weiser, page 429.

[120] Wallace, ibid, Logan's Lament, page 276.

[121] Engels, Jeremy, "Equipped for Murder: The Paxton Boys and the Spirit of Killing All Indians in Pennsylvania, 1763-1764.

[122] Wikipedia.org/wiki/Logan, American Indian leader.

[123] Downes, Council Fires on the Upper Ohio, page 163.

[124] Wallace, Indians in Pennsylvania, page 177.

[125] Downes, Council Fires on the Upper Ohio, page 161.

[126] Wallace, Conrad Weiser, page 276.

[127] Wallace, ibid, page 276.

[128] Downes, Council Fires on the Upper Ohio, page 174.

[129] Blumel, The Zanes: A Frontier Family, page 27.

[130] Blumel, ibid, page 26.

[131] Blumel, ibid, page 36-37.

[132] Hartley, Cecil, Lewis Wetzel, the Virginia Ranger, page 32-33.

[133] Fitzpatrick, Wilderness War on the Ohio, page 417.

[134] Fitzpatrick, ibid, page 431.

[135] Hurt, R. Douglas, The Ohio Frontier, page 89.

[136] Downes, Council Fires on the Upper Ohio, page 271.

[137] Westmoreland County Pennsylvania Genealogy Project, Chapter XXIII, The Slaughter at Gnadenhutten

[138] Withers, Chronicles of Border Warfare, page 324-325.

[139] Archives, Canada, Haldimand Papers, Letters from Officers Commanding at Niagara, Add. Mss. 21762, (B-102), page 14-15.

[140] Archives Canada, HP, ibid, page 43-44.

[141] Archives Canada, HP, ibid, page 87.

[142] Archives Canada, HP, ibid, page 87.

[143] Archives Canada, HP, ibid, page 62.

[144] Archives Canada, HP, ibid, page 72.

[145] Archives Canada, HP, ibid, page 72.

[146] Archives Canada, HP, ibid, page 113.

[147] Archives Canada, HP, Correspondence with lt. Governor Hamilton and papers relating to Detroit, n.d., 1778-1784, MG 21, Add. Mss. 21783 (B-123) page 300.

[148] Archives Canada, HP, Letters from Officers commanding at Niagara, page 113.

[149] Archives Canada, HP, Correspondence and Papers relating to Detroit, page 297.

[150] Archives, Canada, HP, Letters from Officers commanding at Niagara, page 154.

[151] Archives Canada, Return of Persons under the description of Loyalists in Captain Andrew Bradt's Company in the Corps of Rangers, November 30, 1783, MG 21, Add. Mss. 21765, H-1448,

[152] Fitzpatrick, In Their Own Words, page 271.

[153] Blumel, The Zanes: A Frontier Family, page 13.

Index